Wrap, Stitch, Fold & Rivet

Wrap, Stitch, Fold & Rivet

MAKING DESIGNER METAL JEWELRY

Mary Hettmansperger

LARK CRAFTS

A Division of Sterling Publishing Co., Inc.
New York / London

Senior Editor: Marthe Le Van

Editor: Larry Shea

Art Director: Kathleen Holmes

Cover Designer: Cindy LaBreacht

Illustrator: Mary Hettmansperger

Photographer: Stewart O'Shields

Library of Congress Cataloging-in-Publication Data

Hettmansperger, Mary.
   Wrap, stitch, fold & rivet : making designer metal jewelry /
Mary Hettmansperger.
     p.   cm.
   Includes index.
   ISBN-13: 978-1-60059-125-9 (hc-plc with jacket : alk. paper)
   ISBN-10: 1-60059-125-6 (hc-plc with jacket : alk. paper)
   1. Jewelry making.   2. Art metal-work.   I. Title.
TT212.H4635 2008
739.27—dc22

                            2007045193

10 9 8 7 6 5 4

Published by Lark Books, A Division of Sterling Publishing Co., Inc.
387 Park Avenue South, New York, NY 10016

Text © 2008, Mary Hettmansperger
Photos and illustrations © 2008, Lark Books, A Division of
Sterling Publishing Co., Inc, unless otherwise specified

Distributed in Canada by Sterling Publishing, c/o Canadian Manda Group,
165 Dufferin Street, Toronto, Ontario, Canada M6K 3H6

Distributed in the United Kingdom by GMC Distribution Services,
Castle Place, 166 High Street, Lewes, East Sussex, England BN7 1XU

Distributed in Australia by Capricorn Link (Australia) Pty Ltd.,
P.O. Box 704, Windsor, NSW 2756 Australia

If you have questions or comments about this book, please contact:
Lark Books
67 Broadway
Asheville, NC 28801
828-253-0467

Manufactured in China

ISBN 13: 978-1-60059-125-9

For information about custom editions, special sales, premium and corporate
purchases, please contact Sterling Special Sales Department at 800-805-5489 or
specialsales@sterlingpub.com

For information about desk and examination copies available to college and
university professors, requests must be submitted to academic@larkbooks.com.
Our complete policy can be found at www.larkbooks.com.

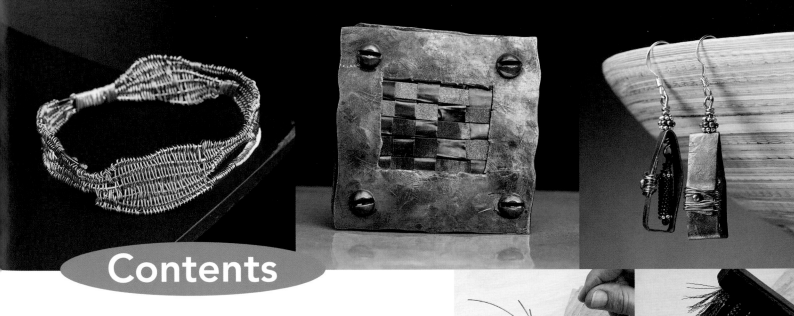

Contents

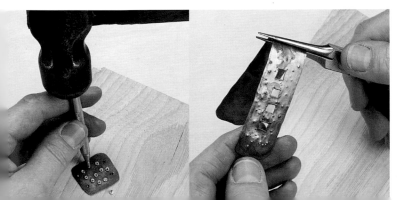

Introduction

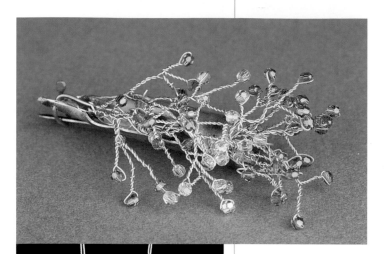

After 25 years of creating art and teaching others how to do it, I've realized that so much of what I do is about making connections. I began my artistic journey through basketry and fiber arts. Weaving, stitching, and connecting are techniques and processes I love. Throughout my weaving years, I always made jewelry using the materials I was working on at the time. (You can see examples of this work in my previous book for Lark, *Fabulous Woven Jewelry*.) Once I discovered metals, I immediately incorporated them into my fiber arts and basketry.

When I started using metal to create jewelry, it was only natural that I treated this material much like the soft fibers I was accustomed to. In my metal jewelry, I have continually found ways—like stitching, folding, and wrapping—to connect pieces without any soldering at all. It's always a challenge to make good connections or embellish a piece using fiber techniques. But I think my ability to draw connections from my work in fiber arts is what enables me to push my metal jewelry into new and exciting territory.

And that's what *Wrap, Stitch, Fold & Rivet* is all about. In this book, I'll show how you can use the techniques I've developed to create unique and stylish metal jewelry right now, without expensive equipment or years of experience. Metal can be an intimidating material to work with, especially in jewelry, where there's an assumption that every piece should be perfect and polished. But today you don't have to be a master metalsmith to create beautiful jewelry. Low-tech applications, everyday materials, and basic tools and finishes make it possible for anyone with a commitment to creativity and a few of the right tools to produce some stunning pieces.

How would I describe the jewelry you'll find in this book? "Natural" is a word I like. This jewelry combines natural materials with many curves, shapes, and textures found in nature. At the same time, the eye and the hand of the artist are always present, whether it's in the interweaving of fine wire or the carefully hammered surface details. These pieces of jewelry have a couple of other things in common. For one thing, you won't need to use solder to make any connections. Also, you won't have to worry about doing things exactly how I tell you to. If you want to change the shape of a component or the materials used, go right ahead. In most of the projects you'll see "Variations" where I did just that. These alternate pieces may contain elements you'd prefer in your own design, or inspire you to create something entirely new.

In the book's Basics section, you'll first learn about the tools—metal and wire cutters, pliers, hammers, and others—that you'll need. We'll then take a spin through the materials you'll work with. Wire and sheeting in silver and copper will be the main components here, accompanied by commercial connections, jewelry findings, and embellishments like beads and found objects. You'll then learn some essential techniques, including a quick course on working with metal—how to cut, forge, texture, and give a patina to this fabulous material. Throughout the Basics section, and again at the end of the book, you'll find a gallery of wonderful works by a number of talented artists who bring their own style to putting metal together into jewelry.

The 20 jewelry projects in the book are divided into four chapters by the techniques highlighted in each piece: simple wraps and folds; commercial connections like nuts, bolts, and eyelets; wire work; and stitching. Projects throughout the book will use several different techniques, enabling you to make connections between them. The Wire-Wrapped Hands Bracelet in the chapter on wire work, for example, also incorporates the unusual commercial connection of small swivels used in fishing tackle.

One thing I've found about working in a creative field like jewelry making is that it gives you the opportunity to make connections in so many ways. I love the connection I make with people who come to my workshops and discover they have the ability to make something they never imagined possible. And everyone who makes jewelry knows the experience of giving a friend or loved one a piece you've created just for her, and strengthening your connection in a special way.

Connections can take you anywhere. A shape, pattern, texture, or design you find striking—on a piece of pottery or clothing, let's say—may be just the inspiration you need to finish a piece of jewelry. My most successful pieces were discovered by accident when I was "playing" in my studio. So feel free to create things without worrying about the resulting product or payoff. It's time to gather your tools and materials, unlock your imagination, and start making connections.

The Basics
Tools

Many craftspeople believe that they can never have too many tools—the more the better—but for me, a few favorites and the simple classics work best. The next few pages present all the basic tools and equipment you'll need to complete the projects in this book, from anvils to wire cutters. As you gain experience, you may want to add those extra tools you find particularly helpful, but you won't require anything more than the tools described here.

Your Workspace

Before getting into the tools you'll need, let's think for a minute about where you're going to be using them. After doing artwork for more than 24 years, I've learned that where and how I work is the key to tapping into creative exploration. I've had a variety of work areas and studio spaces. Recently I acquired a new studio away from my home. This space is not only well lit and ventilated but spacious and accessible. I bring this up not just because I am still in the bragging phase of my move, but also because I think that a good studio/work area must be a priority for any craftsperson.

Your workspace doesn't have to be elaborate or vast, but it does need good light. It should be a safe haven for tools, materials, and artwork. Nothing is more frustrating than having to search for a tool every time you begin working. Try organizing your tools, materials, and supplies so you don't disrupt the creative process.

Some aspects of metalworking—in particular, the intense heat of a torch and the chemical fumes of patina solutions—require special consideration. Ventilation is critical when working on many of the materials needed in the art of jewelry-making. Avoid small, enclosed areas that have no outside air options. I open several windows and use an exhaust fan to move fumes out of and fresh air into my space. If I have to burn any chemicals, I work only outside.

Safety Equipment

When you work with metals, you'll need to take certain precautions. The following items are essential for creating a safe working environment.

• **Safety glasses**—You absolutely must have eye protection when working with metals, since drilling can cause bits of metal to fly off in any direction. You should also wear safety

Safety goggles, safety glasses, work gloves, earplugs, dust mask

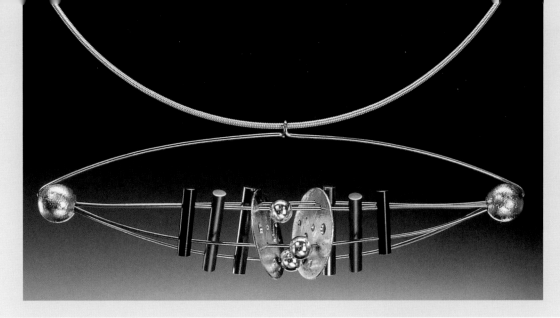

Debra Lynn Gold
Cagey Collar, 2003
4 x 10 x 2 cm
Sterling silver, stainless steel, colored aluminum; pierced, hand-applied distressed finish, tension strung
Photo by Ralph Gabriner

glasses when you're forging metal on an anvil. Normal eyeglasses can't completely protect you, so don't assume they will. Buy safety glasses that fit snugly around your head, blocking the sides of your eyes too.

• **Dust mask and proper ventilation**—Wear a dust mask when filing, drilling, and pounding metals to protect you from inhaling the metal particles. A word of caution: Dust masks do *not* protect against chemical exposure. Always read and follow all directions on patinas and other chemicals you use, and make sure the area is well ventilated.

• **Gloves**—When handling chemicals, always wear rubber or latex gloves to protect your skin. Wear heavy safety gloves to protect your hands from getting injured when you're using a drill on metal. You should also wear gloves when you're forging metal on an anvil. Flexible leather gloves are perfect for this type of work.

• **Ear protection**—Wear ear protection to protect your eardrums when hammering metal on an anvil.

General Tools

You'll use the following items for many tasks when completing the projects in this book, so be sure to keep them on hand.

• **Measuring tape or ruler**—Whenever the project instructions call for you to take a measurement, these are the tools

Rulers, spring clamps, C-clamps

Kim Dolce
Have House, Will Travel, 2007
3.4 x 4 x 0.3 cm
Sterling silver, copper, brass; hand cut, stamped,
hammered, riveted
Photo by artist

Tools for Preparing Metal

When you work with metal, you'll often have to forge wire ends and metal sheeting edges. This process flattens or paddles the wire ends. The edges of metal sheeting, when hammered, spreads to achieve a faceted appearance. You can also create texture with a variety of common jewelry and hardware tools.

Cutting and Holding Tools

There are many tools with a wide range of uses in this category. If you have your own tools that you prefer using, feel free to add them to the list.

Metal Sheet Cutters

These cutters, also known as tin snips, have flat blades that are designed for straight cuts or wide curves, and they leave a clean edge. Many types of cutters are available at a range of prices, but this is one tool I urge you not to skimp on. Purchase metalsmith's or jeweler's quality cutters. The metal snips you find in hardware stores are designed for industrial work. They are not only heavy and hard to use, but they often leave a serrated or rough edge.

Metal sheet cutters

you'll need. You can also use a measuring tape or ruler to check the dimensions of metal shapes and pieces.

• **Adjustable spring clamps**—These rubber-tipped clamps come in handy for holding jewelry parts together as you work. You can also use them to secure metal pieces to the end of a table while you drill. You can purchase adjustable clamps at a hardware or home supply store.

• **C-clamps**—These clamps also secure pieces as you work. Ideal for holding larger pieces, C-clamps have metal tips, so make sure you don't accidentally mar the surface of the piece you're working on.

Wire cutters

Pliers

A versatile tool, **needle-nose pliers** are used for various tasks throughout this book. I prefer the long ones without teeth or ridges. They work well for bending and handling both copper foil and wires. Their smooth surfaces never leave an unwanted mark. Needle-nose pliers work very well for holding metals in a flame, keeping your hand a safe distance from the heat. You can also use them for pulling wire and for bending and shaping metals.

Round-nose pliers are great for making wrapped wire loops. Some advanced wire-working techniques require two pairs of pliers to manipulate the wire, but I use a technique that allows you to use just one pair to create wire loops.

Pliers

Wire Cutters

These are also available in a wide range of prices and styles. I prefer side cutters and end cutters for cutting wire. Both of these types are available from jewelry suppliers and home improvement or hardware stores. They are essential for cutting wire close and clean, and they leave a smooth end.

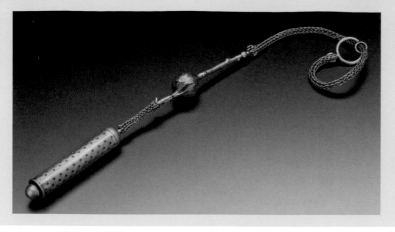

Andrew Latta Kuebeck
Layering Bracelet, 2006
30 x 7 x 2 cm
Copper, patina; electroformed,
fabricated, woven, riveted
Photo by Keith Meiser

Forging Tools

A hammer and anvil are used together for forging. Larger, heavier hammers are effective for forging thicker sheet metals, creating a wonderfully random faceted edge. Try it yourself.

Hammers

Use small hammers to forge the ends of wire and to create a variety of textures on the metal. A ball-peen hammer can make small, round indentations in the metal. You can use a hammer with punching tools such as an awl to create texture and markings on the surface. Use a hammer with eyelet-setting tools to place eyelets. Jewelry hammers and anvils are available from jewelry suppliers, but good-quality hardware store hammers work very well too.

Dapping blocks, ball-peen hammer, punch tools

Anvil

Small anvils can be very helpful for detailed and fine work, but I prefer to use a bench vise from a hardware store for all my jewelry work. A bench vise has an anvil area and a vise you can use to bend sheet metal and make head pins. This tool can be attached securely and directly to your workbench.

Dapping Block

Used with a hammer, this square block can help you shape sheet metal into curved, domed shapes. Place round metal disks into the rounded holes, and then use the round end of a ball-peen hammer or round punch tools to shape the disk, creating a round dome of metal.

Anvil with vise grip, hammers, mallet

Drilling and Punch Tools

When you're working with sheet metal in the projects that follow, you'll drill holes for both functional and decorative purposes. These tools are described here. The basic tools you can find at hardware stores or home supply stores work fine for these purposes. Always wear safety glasses, a dust mask, and gloves when you're drilling metal.

Awl or Ice Pick

This sharply pointed tool (either name will do) has a variety of uses. When drilling in metal sheeting, be sure to use an awl to punch a small pilot hole in the metal, so the drill doesn't slip when you begin drilling. Tap the awl or ice pick with a hammer to punch a hole in the metal or just create texture on the surface.

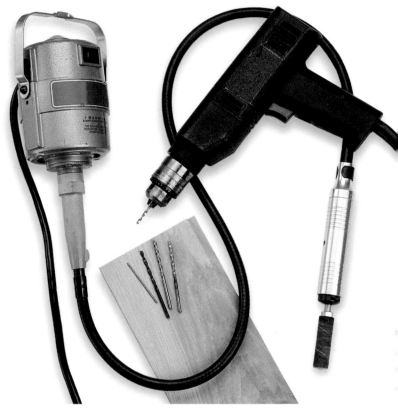

Flexible shaft, hardwood board with drill bits, drill

Awls, ice picks

Drill

To drill through metal, you can use a regular hand-held electric drill or a flexible shaft drill. I also use a drill press for much of my work as it works well for making straight, consistent holes.

The projects in this book require only two drill bit sizes: ⅛ inch (3 mm) and ⅟₁₆ inch (1.6 mm). An ⅛-inch (3 mm) bit makes the exact size hole needed for standard-size eyelets and small nuts and bolts. For brads and holes for stitching and decorative purposes, the ⅟₁₆-inch (1.6 mm) bit size is perfect.

Beth Piver
3 Necklace Beads, 2002
Beads: 5 x 13 x 5 cm
Silver, copper, brass, stainless
steel; hand cut, rolled, riveted
Photo by Jerry Anthony

Hole Punch Tool

A wide variety of tools are available to cut holes into sheet metal using a punch. One popular style is a small screw-hole punch that comes in two sizes. The two metal bars at the top of the tool (which make it resemble a helicopter) turn to punch holes in metal sheeting inserted into the bottom cutting area. This tool does a great job, but my choice for punching holes is a hand-held tool that looks and acts much like a hole punch for paper. Slide a flat metal sheet in the tool, grasp the handle, and squeeze the punch to cut a

hole. Be sure to work carefully because the metal often pops out and can fly in any direction.

Another tool I use to make holes in metal is a basic flat-head screwdriver. I'll discuss how in the following chapter on basic techniques.

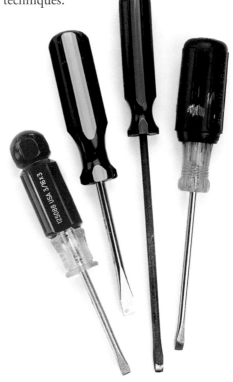

Flat-head screwdrivers

Hole punches

Letter or Stamping Tools

Metal letter sets are fun to use for writing words into your jewelry. They're also useful for marking your jewelry with your initials. You can purchase these tools individually or in full sets of letters and designs.

Adding letters

Letter-stamping set

Carol K. Sakihara
Transparency Brooch, 2007
10.2 x 10.2 x 1.3 cm
Vellum, sterling silver, steel, plastic,
magnet, glue; riveted
Photo by James Obermeier

Finishing Tools

These tools are as versatile as your imagination. Use them in a variety of ways while processing metal pieces and when finishing jewelry.

Metal File

After you've cut metal sheeting into the desired shape, be sure to check for rough edges. File the outside edge with a flat file, and then hammer it to eliminate the sharpness the filing may create. Whenever you cut out windows within the sheeting, file any rough edges with a small, round file. Hammer the metal against the anvil until it's smooth. If you make clean cuts and forge correctly, you often won't have any sharp edges, and you'll be able to skip this step.

Brass or Metal Brush

This is a great tool for adding interesting textures to your jewelry. The metal-bristled brush creates a matte surface on a piece of metal. Brushes can also tone down heavy patinas, taking off some of the application and bringing the metal back to the surface.

Burnishing Tool

When applied to the surface of jewelry, this tool polishes or burnishes the metal. Used with force, it can almost create a mirrored finish. Burnishing tools work best when texture is applied to the surface. This allows the raised area to be burnished or polished and the lower area to remain unchanged.

Eyelet Tool

Follow the directions on the eyelet package to install eyelets. The process is very easy and makes a smooth finish to drilled holes in metal. You can find eyelet tools at scrapbooking, craft, and discount stores.

Tools for Heat Applications and Patinas

The methods you'll use to assemble the pieces in this book are all cold connections—no soldering needed. But you will still need to use a torch in many of the projects to prepare the metal to work with or to create surface treatments.

Propane Torch

A propane torch fitted with a small canister propane tank provides the heat source for the projects. By placing the flame over the copper sheeting or mesh, the heat on metal produces coloration (called flashing). A torch is also used to melt the ends of metal wires to give them a rounded finish. This simple torch produces a large flame that burns fairly clean and hot.

I use the standard tip that comes with the torch as it is the perfect size for the work I do. Smaller tips can actually be too intense for the materials used in the projects here. You can purchase a propane torch and replacement tanks at any home-improvement or hardware store.

Propane torch

From left: files, wire brushes, burnishing tool, eyelet tools

Materials

Most elements of the jewelry in this book are made of metal—in particular, wire and sheeting metal in copper and silver. In this chapter, you'll learn all you need to know about those materials as well as about the other components and embellishments you'll use to create finished pieces.

Wire

Wire is pliable as well as beautiful, making it a natural for connection options in jewelry. The gauge of wire indicates its thickness; the smaller the number, the greater the thickness. Several sizes of wire are used for the projects you'll be making here: relatively fine 26- and 24-gauge wire for weaving and stitching and sturdier 22-, 20-, and 18-gauge wire for making spokes and other structural portions of the jewelry.

Copper, tin-coated, and brass wire can be purchased through metal or jewelry suppliers as well as home-supply and hardware stores. Silver wire is found primarily through jewelry suppliers. Colored and craft wire are available in most craft stores.

Wire Varieties

Copper wire is very pliable and easy to use in all cold-connection applications. Buy bare wire that doesn't have a protective coating or tarnish inhibitor. An aged or tarnished look that develops over time is nice when using copper. You can also speed up the aging process using a patina created by heat or by liver of sulphur.

Silver wire is a beautiful material worth the extra expense. If you're just beginning to use wire in jewelry, you'll find silver wire more difficult to manipulate, weave, and handle than copper since it's less flexible. When you're learning a new technique, try it in copper first to get the feel of it and then use silver.

A less expensive alternative to silver wire is **tin-coated copper wire**. This product has several drawbacks. The wire is not as shiny as silver, has a tendency to darken the skin, and does not turn molten on the ends as nicely as copper and silver wires. With age, it will retain a silver finish, but it does become duller. The great thing about this wire is it responds much like the bare copper wire, so it is relatively easy to handle. This aged effect works particularly well with found objects.

Both **brass and colored craft** wire in smaller gauges are practical for weaving applications in small jewelry projects.

Assorted wires

Eleanore Macnish
Roman Chicken, 2006
9 x 7.2 x 0.5 cm
Brass, fur, plastic watch crystal, ceramic chicken,
Victorian cutout, malachite, sterling silver, Bakelite, dye;
hand cut, cold connected, riveted, bezel set malachite
Photo by Margo Geist

I also use some of the larger-gauge craft wires in wrapped loops. However, neither of these wires reacts well to the heat of the torch, and craft wires have a tendency to lose their colored finish over time from wear.

Wire Treatments

You can give copper and silver wire an array of patina applications. The projects in this book call for liver of sulphur and heat-treated patinas to darken or age the wire. You can forge larger-gauge wires (that is, thicker wires with a lower gauge number) on the ends with a hammer and anvil to flatten or paddle them flat. Heat-treating the ends of the wire with a torch results in the end becoming molten hot and consequently balling up.

Metal Sheeting

The metal used for the projects here is primarily copper and silver. Brass sheeting is used in small accents here and there throughout the projects. The copper and brass sheeting used is 24-gauge due to its versatility. I use a wider range of gauges of silver sheeting, though I most often use finer sheets of silver both for ease of use and lower expense.

Copper

Copper materials are among my favorites for making all styles of jewelry. They are inexpensive and readily available. Over time, copper materials turn a darker coppery color, eliminating any harsh shiny effect. When you apply a torch to copper to produce a patina, a variety of colors appears on the surface. These colors range from yellows and pinks to dark purples, reds, and oranges, which are much more vibrant than the aged look.

Copper sheeting is malleable. You can easily drill it, cut it into a variety of shapes, texture it, and forge it. All the projects that use copper sheeting in this book call for 24-gauge because it is rigid but easy to cut. As with copper wire, you can add a patina by applying heat to it, which will bring out a wide range of colors and effects. You can also deckle the edges by forging them.

Copper foil is a thin sheet metal that varies in thickness. It is extremely easy to use and manipulate, making it perfect to weave with. You can cut it with scissors or fold and bend it with needle-nose pliers. The Woven Windows Pin project on page 63 uses .002-width copper foil for the woven grid. You can order copper foil through metal or jewelry suppliers, and some craft and hardware stores carry it as well.

Copper mesh is woven wire cloth that makes a nice textural addition to jewelry. My favorite size to use is 100 x 100 mesh per inch.

Lisa Crowder
Double Oval Necklace,
2007
5.1 x 40.6 x 1.3 cm
Sterling silver; hand fabricated, riveted, oxidized
Photo by Hap Sakwa

Silver

As you progress through the book, you'll use **silver sheet-ing** in a variety of ways. I use dead soft sterling silver sheeting because of the ease of working it. For layering, small projects, folds, and wraps, 30-gauge sterling sheeting works best. It is soft enough to achieve a nice texture, and once it is forged and worked hard, it becomes a nice, strong piece of silver for jewelry designs. A few projects call for 24-gauge sterling silver sheeting because of its weight and strength.

You can torch silver sheeting much like copper, but use a lower flame and do not allow the sheet to become over-heated. Silver melts at a faster rate than copper, so you can ruin it quickly. Silver's color variations are different than those of copper, resulting in more gold colors, yellows, browns, and purples.

Stainless mesh is beautiful to use when making silver jewelry, but I like to use it in a finer grade than copper mesh due to the stiff quality of the material. A perfect size in stainless to bend, cut, and manipulate is 160 x 160 mesh per inch.

Copper foil; brass, silver, and copper sheeting; copper and stainless mesh

Commercial Connections

Commercial connections refer to manufactured items. Look through bins at a hardware store, and let your imagination roam. Scrapbook stores have endless items that can be used in the cold-connection process. Try to stick to metal items, and avoid plastic, cardboard, or fragile materials. Many items and materials can be adapted to jewelry, and they're available through a variety of sources—craft supply stores, beading suppliers, fabric shops, scrapbooking and hardware stores, flea markets, electronic and salvage outlets, and antiques stores to name just a few.

Nuts, Bolts, and Rivets

Use small nuts and bolts in brass, stainless, and copper—which you can easily find at your local hardware store—to connect layers of metal sheeting. You can even find miniature-size nuts and bolts through jewelry, electronic, and hobby resources. I often put a drop of glue on the threads of the nut just before I make the connection to assure the bolt will not screw out over time. Rivets can also hold two pieces of sheet metal together; you fasten them by hammering the back side of the rivet. That spreads the metal rivet out and creates a lip that secures the rivet in place.

From left: nuts, bolts, rivets

Eyelets and Brads

You can finish the edges of drilled holes in metal by inserting eyelets into them. These small tube-shaped pieces have a rolled edge or lip on one end. That allows you to spread the back side open and retains the hole in the metal. Eyelets are available in many colors and finishes at craft, scrapbooking, and fabric stores. A tool for mounting comes with the eyelets, which can also be used to connect two pieces of metal.

Brads can be found in office supply stores, scrapbook retailers, and hardware stores. Brads have a head on one end that is plain or decorative. From the back side of the head are two metal spikes that insert into a drilled or punched hole. The spikes are separated and folded back on the metal, which secures the head of the brad in place. I use these when I am going to layer metals.

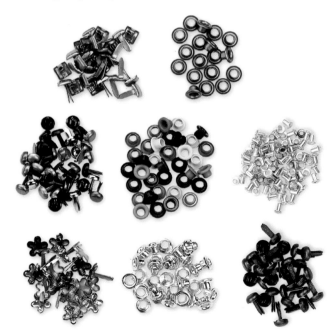

Assorted brads and eyelets

Meghan O'Rourke
Titanium Bracelets, 2007
Left, 9 x 9 x 1 cm; right,
11 x 11 x 2 cm
Titanium, sterling silver,
18-karat gold; hand cut,
chased, anodized, riveted
Photo by Grant Hancock

Jewelry Findings and Components

Metal jewelry findings—such as pin backs, stickpins, neck chains, clasps, toggles, and ear wires—finish a piece of jewelry so you can wear it. Findings come in a variety of metals, everything from 14-karat gold and sterling to hypoallergenic and base metals. The goal is to find the finding that suits the piece of jewelry you're making. Keep in mind that some alloys can tarnish and dull over time and often darken the skin, and some people are allergic to base metals, especially in ear wires that pierce the skin. A precious metal is often well worth the extra expense.

Neck Chains

Using a combination of silver, brass, copper, beads, and found items in jewelry gives you a wide range of choices for matching neck chains. If a silver or copper chain is too bright and shiny for a rustic piece, the chain can easily be antiqued or darkened with liver of sulphur.

You can purchase chains by the foot then buy clasps separately and add them. This makes odd lengths an option. You can also buy neck chains complete with clasps and ready to wear. I prefer standard chains, usually 20 or 24 inches (50.8 or 61 cm) in length. Choker-style hangers are good choices for focal pieces as in the Twisted Wire Choker

Necklace project on page 118. Whatever style, metal, or length of chain you choose, all are available at jewelry supply stores.

Clasps

Clasps are attached to neck chains and bracelets to make the connection secure. Basic **spring-ring clasps** work well for most pieces. They are made of a ring with a small lever that, when pulled back, opens the clasp, and they're most common for neck chains.

Toggle clasps consist of two parts and are mainly used for bracelet connections. One piece is attached to each end of a bracelet. One half of the toggle is a bar or narrow, elongated shape. The other half is a loop big enough for the bar to pass through, so when it is turned crosswise it will hold tight.

A **slide clasp**, another common bracelet connection, consists of two tube-shaped bars, each having one capped end and one open end. One of the bars is slightly smaller than the other and has a small metal spring catch on one side of the tube. The other side of the tube has a series of soldered rings or bars to attach to the bracelet. The larger bar has a similar series of soldered rings or bar, but it has a slit along its opposite side to allow the smaller tube to slide in. This clasp is particularly good for making bracelets that have several strands in the design.

Stickpins

Stickpins are long pins for brooches that have a little flat, round metal piece on one end and the point of the pin at the other end. This flat disk makes it possible to attach it with glue or secure it inside metal layers onto the back of a piece of jewelry.

Bar Pin Backs

These pin backs have a flat, elongated piece of metal on the back that attaches to the piece of jewelry and a long pin for piercing through clothing and fitting into a clasp that closes

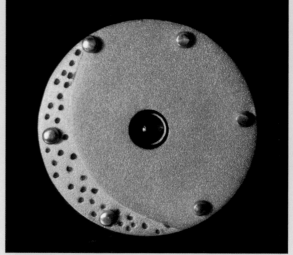

Victoria Altepeter
Galactic Brooch, 2007
2.5 x 2. X 0.6 cm
Sterling silver, 24-karat gold, fine silver, garnet;
tube-set, kum boo
Photo by artist

on the other end. Some styles have three holes in the flat metal backing that make it possible to sew them to the back of a piece. Other styles have a straight solid bar that connects directly to the piece of jewelry and is soldered to make it adhere.

Jump Rings

Jump rings are wire circles with splits and are used to connect various parts of jewelry. They are available in a variety of metals, such as gold, silver, plated gold and silver, pewter, brass, copper, and base metal.

Ear Wires

Ear wires are attached to earrings so that they can be worn. Purchasing ear wires in sterling silver or a hypoallergenic metal ensures there will be no allergic reaction to the metal. Copper ear wires are also a great-looking choice, but not everyone can wear them.

Neck chains, neck cable, jump rings, stickpins, bar pin backs, spring-ring clasps, copper sister hook, toggle clasp, ear wires, watch

Embellishments

The pieces of jewelry in this book are mostly made of metal—either wire or sheeting. But several of them incorporate other materials as embellishments or accents.

Beads

Beads are used in the projects as embellishments to a piece of jewelry, to accent the connection process, or on a head pin to create a bangle. As you make jewelry, you'll find yourself collecting beads since they come in so many colors and finishes.

Bead, craft, and fabric stores all carry beads. I like to use a variety of metal beads in my jewelry. When you're thinking about beads for a project, be sure that the holes are large enough to thread onto wire gauge you plan to use. Most beads are measured in millimeters, with the size referring to the diameter of the bead.

Found Objects

Found objects can add visual interest to your jewelry. Swivels (a type of fishing tackle) become a functional part of the Wire-Wrapped Hands Bracelet on page 94. Antique coins, foreign coins, and bus tokens can make an interesting layer in designing.

You can successfully incorporate found objects by making them an integral part of the design. Changing the shape, surface, or function always makes found objects more interesting. By using found objects in jewelry, you remove them from their usual context, lending your pieces an unconventional look.

I use all kinds of bottle caps in jewelry—whether they're old ones that I've found or new ones purchased from craft or scrapbooking stores. Rusted caps give you a nice surface to work with, but they need to be cleaned first with soap, water, and a wire brush. Always wear a dust mask to avoid inhaling

Assorted beads

Found objects

small rust particles. After they're dry, apply non-yellowing matte fixative to the smoothed surface. After the cap dries, test the finish by rubbing it with a clean white cloth.

In one project, you'll need to drill holes in bottle caps for the lid pin. Caps fitted with rubber seals are great for drilling because the rubber helps hold the piece in place. If you're using a found lid or cap with no rubber seal, put on safety glasses, and punch small holes with your awl and hammer before drilling. When you do the drilling, protect your hands with heavy gloves, such as ones made of leather.

Other Materials
Here are other materials you will need to create certain projects in this book.

Glues and Fixatives
Some projects use particular glues and adhesives to attach components. Be sure to read and carefully follow the manufacturer's directions when using any glue or epoxy.

From left: quick-drying glue, two-part epoxy, spray fixative, industrial adhesive

Use non-yellowing spray matte fixative to help hold a heavy patina. You can use fixative as a sealant for copper sheeting, mesh, and foil to help retain the color of the patina. To use a fixative on found objects, spray a thin, light coat, which seals the surface and helps prevent them from flaking.

Irish Waxed Linen and Cords
You can use a variety of cords—such as ribbon, leather, or hemp—as part of necklaces or other jewelry items. Waxed linen is my favorite material for making neck cords due to its strength (I use the 4-ply variety) and ease in making simple cordage. It can be purchased from basketry, bead, and bookbinding suppliers.

Chemical Patinas
Some patinas are applied to metal through heat while others require a chemical solution. In a later chapter, Working with Metal, I'll discuss how to create patina with conventional materials such as liver of sulphur as well as with an unconventional one.

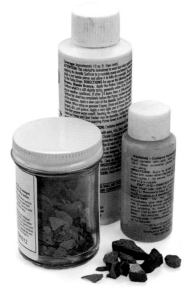

From left: liver of sulphur, patina green antiquing solution, black patina solution

Basic Techniques

I said earlier that I like to use simple, basic tools for making jewelry. In most cases, I also use simple techniques that are easy to learn and do. This chapter covers some basic ways to set eyelets, cut holes, wrap wires, and do other processes.

Drilling, Punching, and Cutting Holes

When you punch or drill metal, clear off your worktable so that you have plenty of room. Place a scrap of flat wood underneath the metal to protect the table's top surface from the drill bit. A hardwood, such as hickory or oak, will hold up longer than a softer wood. Secure the metal piece with a vice or clamp. If the piece of metal is small and hard to clamp, you can wear a heavy leather glove while holding the metal piece. Always wear eye protection and a dust mask, and make sure the metal piece is secure before you drill.

When I first learned to work with metal, I used a saw to cut holes in my sheet metal, but after breaking many blades I decided to try something different. I like simple square and triangle shapes for windows in my pieces. As barbaric as this may seem, I found that if I take a flat-head screwdriver and sharpen the flat area, it becomes a great cutting device. I place the sharpened edge where I want to cut, hammer the end of the handle, and pierce through the sheeting. Long open areas can be created by moving the screwdriver along the line you are cutting to extend the hole.

Drilling a hole

Punching holes

Cutting a hole with a screwdriver

John Rose
This Modern Life, 2007
Each: 7 x 2.2 x 0.6 cm
Aluminum, bronze; hand forged, milled
Photo by artist

Setting Eyelets

This application is one of the last things done to a piece of jewelry to avoid damaging the eyelet once it is in place. Place the eyelet inside the hole, with the large rim edge to the front side of your piece. Place the eyelet tool in the small circle on the back side, and hammer the tool to spread out the tube shape that will secure the eyelet in place.

For more information on specific eyelets, follow the manufacturer's instructions on the insert for the eyelet tool.

Setting an eyelet

Wire Wrapping

To make jewelry connections without using heat, wire wrapping is a great technique. The following sections describe the steps you take to create a variety of wire elements.

Making Wire-Wrapped Loops

I like to make a wrapped loop that is a teardrop shape. This is not the traditional method, but it is what I use for most of my wire work. Here's how to do it.

1. Hold the wire with the pliers where you want to create the loop.

2. Pull the wire around one of the tips on the pliers to make the desired loop size, ending at a 90° angle.

3. Reposition the pliers to hold the loop.

4. Take the end of the wire at 90°, and wrap tightly and consistently away from the loop.

Janice Berkebile
Lilies and Leaves #1, 2006
36 x 4 x 2 cm
Sterling silver, copper, semiprecious beads;
fused, hand textured
Photo by artist

Wrapped loops have a great variety of types and functions that you can take advantage of in making jewelry. For example:

As shown here, you can achieve a variety of wrapped loops by changing the shapes and sizes of the loops.

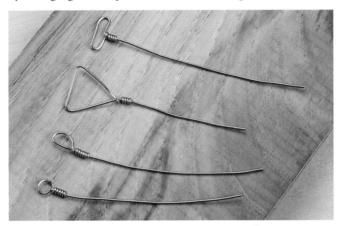

Wrapped loops can connect with one another.

5. Cut close with flush wire cutters. Crimp the wire around tightly with pliers to avoid any sharp ends.

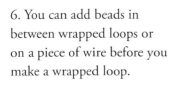

6. You can add beads in between wrapped loops or on a piece of wire before you make a wrapped loop.

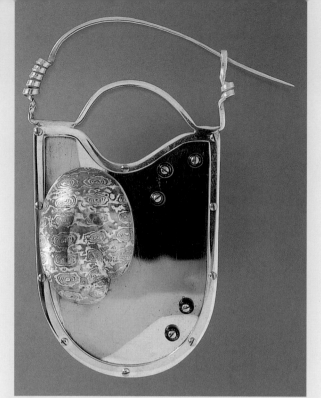

Patricia M. Wierman
Planetary Shield Fibula, 1993
9.4 x 7 x 1 cm
Sterling silver, copper, mokume-gane, nuts, bolts, glass
beads; fabricated forged, married metal, repoussé,
chased, drilled, cold connected
Photo by Daniel V. Wierman

Loops can also be used for the finish wire to hold a
neck chain.

Traditional Wrapped Loop

Here's the more commonly used method for creating
wrapped loops. Use whichever one works best for you.

1. Using pliers, begin the wrapped
loop by bending the wire or a head
pin to form a right angle where the
loop will be made.

2. With your round-nose pliers,
position the bottom tip of the pliers at the right of the bend you just
created. Then, pull the wire over
the top of the round-nose pliers.

3. Reposition the round-nose pliers.
Now place the bottom tip of the pliers
inside the curve (where the loop will
be). Pull the end of the wire under the
bottom of the round-nose pliers.

4. Reposition your pliers, holding
the loop. Use your fingers or chain-
nose pliers to wrap the end of the
wire around the wire stem. Make
several wraps, and cut off the excess
wire at an angle and as close as you
can. Use chain-nose pliers to press
the cut end to avoid any sharp ends.

Wrapped Loop Swirl Charm

This swirling piece of wire is easy to create, and it makes for a nice decorative element in your jewelry.

1. Using round-nose pliers, grasp the end of a 5-inch (12.7 cm) piece of wire, and pull the opposite end around to make a circle, working it flat.

2. Continue to make the circle, increasing the size of the circle to allow for space in between the wire as you increase in size. You can do this with the pliers or your fingers.

3. Stop the swirl of wire at the desired size. With the pliers, bend the wire at a 90° angle. Make a wrapped loop with this wire to create a charm.

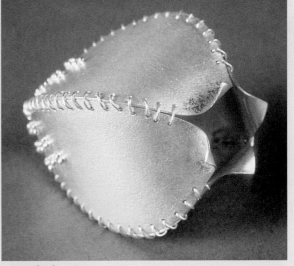

Nisa Blackmon
Maturation Series: IV, 1994
3.2 x 3.2 x 5 cm
Sterling silver, fine silver wire; textured, formed, granulated, sewn
Photo by artist

You can use this wire technique to create charms in a variety of shapes.

Once the charm is complete, forge the swirl and stem area to make it work hard.

Head Pin and Beads with Wrapped Loops

Commercial head pins, paddled wire, or wire with melted ends to form balls can all be used as head pins to hold beads and embellish your pieces.

First, thread beads on the wire, and allow them to stop at the larger end of the headpin.

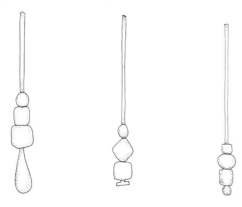

Finish the beaded head pins with any of the wrapped-loop methods mentioned above at the top of the wire.

Hiding Ends for Wrapping Wire

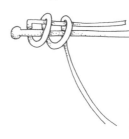

1. Wrap a piece of wire (24-gauge or smaller) over a solid core. Hold the end of the 24-gauge wire alongside the core piece. Make a loop with the wire, and then begin wrapping the wire over itself.

2. Firmly wrap in a neat and consistent manner. After about four wraps, pull the end of the loop to secure it.

3. Cut the end of the loop wire, and continue to wrap, covering the end.

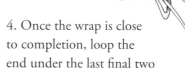

4. Once the wrap is close to completion, loop the end under the last final two or three wraps.

5. Pull the end of the wire's loop, and the final wraps will secure.

6. Cut the end, and push it under the wraps to hide it.

Cody Bush
Dangerboy Bracelet, 1997
70 x 70 x 2.5 cm
Brass, aluminum, patina; anodized, pop riveted
Photo by artist

Using Jump Rings and Ear Wires

To use both of these findings, slide the split in the circle from side to side with two pliers. Do not open the circle by pulling it apart. This loosens the circle shape and can weaken the metal.

Opening jump rings

Working with Metal

In this chapter, you will get a crash course in beginning metalwork. The processes explained here barely touch on the immense amount of available information in the field of metalwork. As an artist, I come from a fiber background, so my approaches to connections, jewelry design, and metal applications are not the same as those of traditional jewelers. The fire scale that traditional jewelers try to avoid on the surface of metal is something I tend to celebrate. The stitch that I use to connect two pieces of metal would instead be soldered by a serious metalsmith. Keep in mind the projects in this book are rustic, altered, and organic.

Using a Torch

A propane torch is the main heat application you'll use in this book to prepare metal surfaces for patinas, textures, and forging. The torch is a vital tool in obtaining successful patinas. Moving a copper piece in and out of the flame results in beautiful colors, swirls, and patterns. You'll also use the torch to anneal copper to make it more pliable and to prepare the metal for textures, shaping, and forging.

Copper and stainless mesh, as well as copper foil, react in the same way as metal sheeting in the flame. These finer-gauge materials color more quickly because they are thinner. Don't overheat these thin metals, or you might burn holes through them. Silver melts faster than copper, so be sure not to overheat.

Assortment of colored metal

Annealing

Annealing metal is a heat treatment where the material is altered, weakening its properties (such as strength and hardness) to make it more workable. This is a process where you use the torch to heat the metal, allow it to remain in the heat until it is molten hot or glowing, and then cool it.

Heating the metal with a torch

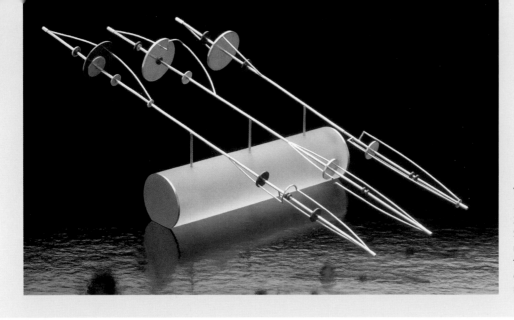

Tom Muir
Stickpins, 1983
21 x 11.4 x 6.4 cm
Stainless steel, sterling silver,
nickel silver, plexiglass,
titanium; fabricated, cold
connected
Photo by Rob Wheless

Either air-drying or a cold-water quench gives the material the same flexibility for working with it as copper. Annealing redefines the structure, relieves internal stresses, and induces softness. Once the metal is annealed, it becomes easier

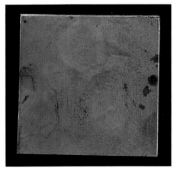

Red annealed copper

to shape, form, cut, or texture. Another positive effect of annealing: When copper is annealed before applying patinas, patination will be more successful due to the changes that the copper has undergone.

Fire Scale

Holding a piece of metal too long in the flame can blacken it, causing fire scale to occur. Fire scale is caused by oxygen combining with copper during the torching process. Due to its copper content, sterling silver has a tendency to form fire scale during both soldering and annealing. When silversmiths solder, they cover the sterling silver with a protective coating (a boric acid base), so the oxygen cannot reach the surface during the heating process. The gauges of sterling silver sheeting used for the projects in this book are quite thin, and you will need to use caution at all times with your flame to avoid melting the silver. When fire scale metal is forged, textured, or punched with lettering or tools, some

of the fire scale will disappear. The change in the metal after fire scale can enhance any applications made to the metal.

Fire scale

Judith Hoyt
Mild and Mellow Brooch, 2005
7.6 x 5.7 cm
Found metal, copper, stainless steel, oil paint; riveted
Photo by John Lenz

You can count on copper forming fire scale when heated, and there are many ways to approach this issue. You can remove fire scale by using a brass brush on the surface, polishing, or filing the black coat off to expose the metal below. Many metalsmiths use a pickle solution (an acidic liquid or powder diluted with water in a container) to clean their work and reduce oxides on the copper. I rarely use a pickle pot because I like the aged and rustic look I achieve by reheating the copper instead of cleaning it. By reheating the copper and placing it in ice-cold water, you can reduce the oxygen it is exposed to, which in turn reduces the fire scale. This oxidation process will often redden the surface permanently—a look you may want to try for in some of the projects. To accomplish this, take a piece of copper and

hold it in the flame until you see it is molten hot and has a glow. At that point, immediately pull the piece out of the flame and quench it in cold or iced water. This is a cold-water patina. Since the jewelry I create has an altered art look, I like the rustic and relic looks that the copper takes on from this heat and cold water application. Red coloration is achieved and maintained throughout a variety of applications to the copper.

Heat Applications for Wire

You can finish the cut end of a piece of copper or silver wire by heating it up in the flame of the torch. This will cause the end to melt, forming a ball as the metal melts upon itself.

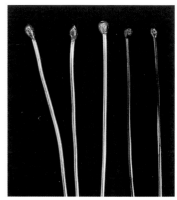

Place the end of the wire in the flame, and allow the metal to melt and sag slightly. Pull it from the flame when the end is shaped into a round ball.

Balls on wire

If copper wire is removed from the flame at the melting point and put directly into icy or very cold water, it develops a bright red-pink color—a cold-water patina that's permanent. If the wire is allowed to air-dry instead of cooling

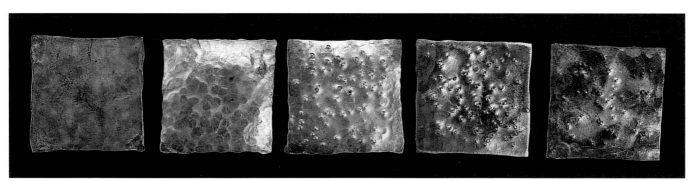

Examples of heat applications and forging to achieve color and texture

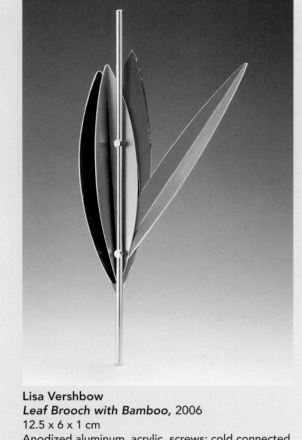

Lisa Vershbow
Leaf Brooch with Bamboo, 2006
12.5 x 6 x 1 cm
Anodized aluminum, acrylic, screws; cold connected
Photo by Munch Studio

in water, it will turn black. If you burn the ends of silver wire and cool them in cold water, they'll turn pale pink. If you torch the ends of tin-coated wire, they'll turn red-bright pink like bare copper. Always burn the tin-coated wire outdoors because of the dangerous fumes released from the tin coating.

Silver wire reacts the same way. However, be sure to hold the wire down into the flame to create a round ball. Silver has a tendency to slump to one side if it is held above the flame.

Patinas and Textures

Patina can refer to any fading, darkening, or other signs of age, whether they are natural or intentionally produced. Patina is generally a chemical compound formed on the surface of metal from exposure to the elements and time. Artists and metalsmiths deliberately add chemical patinas to the surface of metal to rust, age, darken, or color an object. The chemical process by which a patina forms is called *patination*, and a work of art coated by a patina is said to be *patinated*. Many patinas are temporary and sit only on the surface of the metal; they can change or flake off. Other patinas have changed the metal and remain permanent.

Patinas on Copper and Silver Sheeting

Always prepare the copper for patinas by first heating it, which allows the patina to react more easily to the metal. You can also forge and texture copper before applying the patinas, especially if you do not want the patina disturbed or altered once it is applied. If the metal has been worked hard, textured, or heated prior to adding patinas to its surface, the patina is achieved faster and with more success. If the metal is new, smooth, unworked, or unheated, it has a tendency to resist the patina. The common green patina that forms on the surface of copper is created by slow chemical alteration of the copper, producing a basic carbonate.

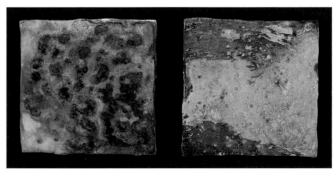

Green patinas

Sim Luttin
Departure from Nature, 2005
Each: 5 cm in diameter
Sterling silver, 14-karat yellow gold, mild steel, copper, patina; hand cut, cold connected, pressed
Photo by Kevin Montague

This green surface texture can form on pure copper objects as well as alloys that contain copper, such as bronze or brass. The green patina is a result of weather, elements, and water exposure. On the other hand, silver will tarnish over time, turning a muddy gray color and becoming dull.

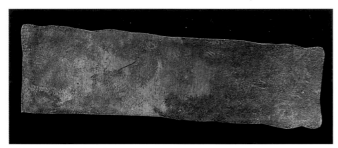

Silver tarnished dark

You can patinate copper to achieve the green coloration by using a green patina solution that speeds up the process.

Yellow patina on silver

The chlorides in these products lead to the green coloration. Using a matte fixative helps adhere the surface, chalky green to teal blue, to the metal and keep it from flaking off. When you apply the green patina solution to silver, you achieve a lighter yellow-gold color.

A wide range of chemicals and materials, both household and commercial, can produce a variety of patinas. Sulphur compounds (such as liver of sulphur) are exceptionally nice to work with due to the variety of hues that you achieve if you monitor them carefully. If the metal sheeting is over-exposed to the liquid, it tends to brown and even blacken. Liver of sulphur comes in a rock form; you prepare it for use by placing a small piece of the rock in hot or boiling water where it dissolves. Make sure the container you are using to make the bath is not metal and is not used

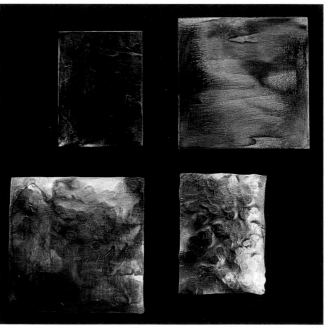

Pieces colored with liver of sulphur

Tana Acton
Asymmetrica 3-D with Stones, 2006
4.4 x 8.3 x 6.4 cm
Ocean stones, sterling silver, nickel; wrapped
Photo by Larry Sanders

Many factors affect how the piece will react to the patina. How much the metal has been worked, the gauge of the copper or silver, and the texture you have on the piece all factor in.

An application of lemon juice can also speed up the aged look for copper and silver. The copper darkens to a rich, deep brown wherever the lemon juice makes contact. Using a spray bottle with lemon juice on copper creates subtle spots and patterns where the mist of the liquid lands.

You can apply silver-black (hydrochloric acid) to silver or copper. It immediately blackens both metals.

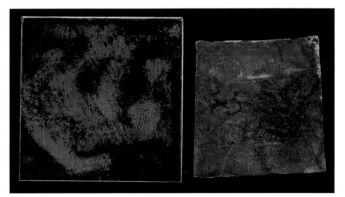

Silver-black patina

for cooking. A rotten-egg sulphur fume will be present, so make sure your area is well ventilated when using this patina. Dipping the copper or silver in the solution starts the patina process. Dip the metals into the sulphur bath; go in and out very quickly, and watch the entire time what reaction is occurring. Make sure you monitor the coloration as you dip the metal. Minimal exposure and monitoring the coloration can lead to brilliant purples, reds, and yellows on both silver and copper.

Liver of sulphur is commonly used by jewelry artists to both age a piece and darken crevices of a piece to enhance detail. By buffing or reworking the metal, you can bring back the shine to the surface, leaving the recessed areas of the piece dark.

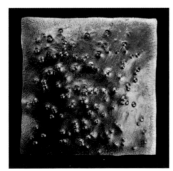

Textured and highlighted copper

Polishing, cleaning, tumbling, and burnishing blackened metal can bring out the metal below the patina, adding depth and detail. Keep in mind that a neck chain, jump rings, copper and silver wires, and findings can also take a patina from any of the above methods and products.

Heat and Patinas

Copper and silver patination can be deliberately accelerated by using heat after you have applied the patina. Using a torch with the patina products speeds up the process and changes the results. Heat often brings out more vibrant coloration than you can achieve without it.

Using a torch with patina products should only be done in open air or a ventilated area so as not to inhale any of the chemical fumes. Hold the metal with old pliers, and move the piece of metal in and out of the flame of the torch. The colors created will range from greens, yellows, and oranges to deep blues, reds, and purples depending on the patina used. You can reapply patina solutions and repeat the process, or once applied leave them to air-dry and process.

Years ago, totally by accident, I discovered a very nontraditional patina. I spilled dry cat food on copper foil I was about to patina with the torch. Instead of pushing it off the surface, I went ahead and torched the foil with the cat food on it. What I discovered is that the oil in the cat food keeps the pieces from moving on the surface, and they smolder as the heat radiates around the food, creating amazing colors. It's a fun technique, so give it a try.

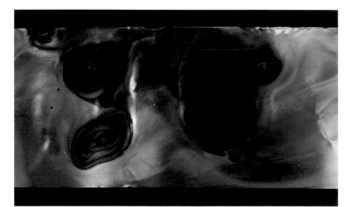

Cat food patina

Preparing Sheet Metals

By annealing the metal first, the process of forging, texturing, and shaping the metal will be easier due to the soft quality of the metal after it is heated. However, it is not mandatory that you process the metal in heat first. Either approach is fine, and trying both will allow you to decide what results you prefer.

Forging Metals

In some of the projects, you will forge the edges of cut sheet metal with a hammer and anvil to smooth them out and create a deckled edge. I like the organic quality of the edge obtained by this process. Hammering the metal also makes it work hard, a term that relates to the strength and stiffness the metal will take on as you work with it.

As you forge the metal, allow the hammer to do the work. Position the head so that it will strike the area you're forging. Allow it to gain momentum as you swing it to disperse the weight and get optimum force. With practice you'll gain expertise and do this with ease.

Deckled copper edge

Beth Piver
Bunnyman Brooch, 2005
9.5 x 6 x 1 cm
Silver, copper, bronze, brass, steel, acrylic paint;
hand cut, etched, painted, cold connected
Photo by Jerry Anthony

Wire can also be forged or hammered flat. By flattening just the cut ends of the wire, paddles take shape.

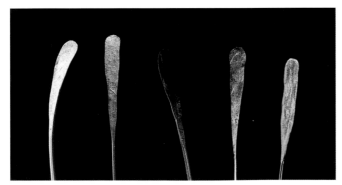

Paddles with wire

You can form piece of wire into a shape and then hammer it. Since the wire has been worked hard by the forging process, the shape is now stiff, and the wire is no longer pliable. This is a great way to create your own swirls and shapes.

Wrapped hammer shapes

Keep in mind that the wire will weaken if you hammer it out too thinly, so don't overdo it or the wire will become brittle. Balls that you've created on the ends of the wire can also be hammered flat.

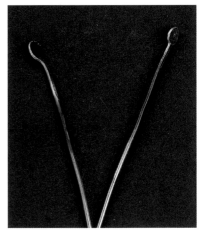

Balls hammered flat

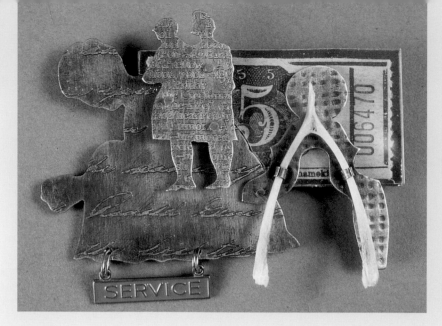

Nisa Blackmon
Community Chest, 1993
6.3 x 7.5 x 1 cm
Copper, red brass, yellow brass, acrylic, found objects; etched, roller printed, riveted
Photo by artist

Texturing Metals

Applying a texture or surface to metal can be a nice addition to the metal pieces you work with. One of my favorite texture techniques is to use a blunt awl tip on the metal. Use the tool by hammering its handle gently at first to see what indentation you achieve.

Gauge, kind, and condition of the metal all play a role in acquiring a texture. Once you have established how the tools, the metal, and your skill level react with each other, you can let your creative juices flow.

Other tools such as a flathead screwdriver once sharpened can make an easy cut for a window. Any punch or letter-stamp tool can also add texture and words to your metal.

Brass brushes, files, and grinding tools can give the metal subtle textures and surfaces.

Texturing with an awl

Before You Get Started

Before you make the projects in the book, it's a good idea to get more familiar with some of the techniques described here. Try putting a patina on and then applying texture or vice versa. Playing with the options in texturing, forging, and adding patinas can be an art in itself. You may approach all of these techniques in a variety of ways. Always be safe, using a well ventilated or open-air area. Safety glasses, dust mask, gloves, and ear protection are all safety tools that you should always use when appropriate.

A final note: Make sure you clean up the back sides of your finished pieces with a brass brush or cleaner, so the fire scale, patinas, and torch applications do not darken skin or clothing.

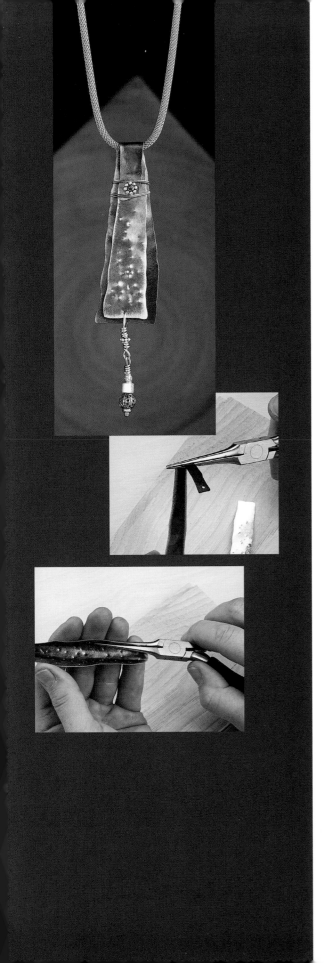

The Projects

CHAPTER 1
Wraps and Folds

"Organic" might be the right word to describe the layers of metal shapes, folds, and unexpected twists and wraps that make up the jewelry in this chapter. These five projects allow a beginner in metalworking—like you, perhaps—to become comfortable using a torch and some basic tools. Once you're familiar with the technical evolution of the pieces, it will be easier to expand on the concepts to create unique work in your own style.

Each project in this chapter begins with flat pieces of sheet metal cut into specific shapes and either stacked, wrapped, or folded. Several projects introduce you to applying heat patinas to the copper or silver sheet to give the metal an aged look and some variation in color. You'll create texturing with a hammer or other workbench tools. You'll find that employing simple wire and bead techniques adds even more surface detail and interest.

The first project is a necklace composed of layers of cut and textured shapes, giving you a chance to work with many of the materials and tools that you'll use throughout the book. The wrapped loop bail connection offers plenty of space to add as many layers as you wish to your necklace.

A series of folds creates the earrings in the second project. Pre-designing the placement of both the folds and holes allows you to assemble the earrings by simply bending and attaching the beads. The Bead Shelf Necklace, the next project, transforms a flat, rectangular shape into a wonderful three-dimensional piece of jewelry. The fourth project in the chapter makes use of any and all of the earlier cold-connection techniques. This necklace may well be the most creative and self-expressive in the book. The necklace in the last project, a simple wrap of silver sheeting around beads, incorporates the intriguing detail of partial beads showing through the opening.

Stacking, arranging, and designing pieces of cut metal into small pieces of art is truly satisfying. Two pieces made this way never come out completely the same. Even if you do not consider yourself an artist of jewelry (yet!), the projects that follow will inspire you and ignite your creativity.

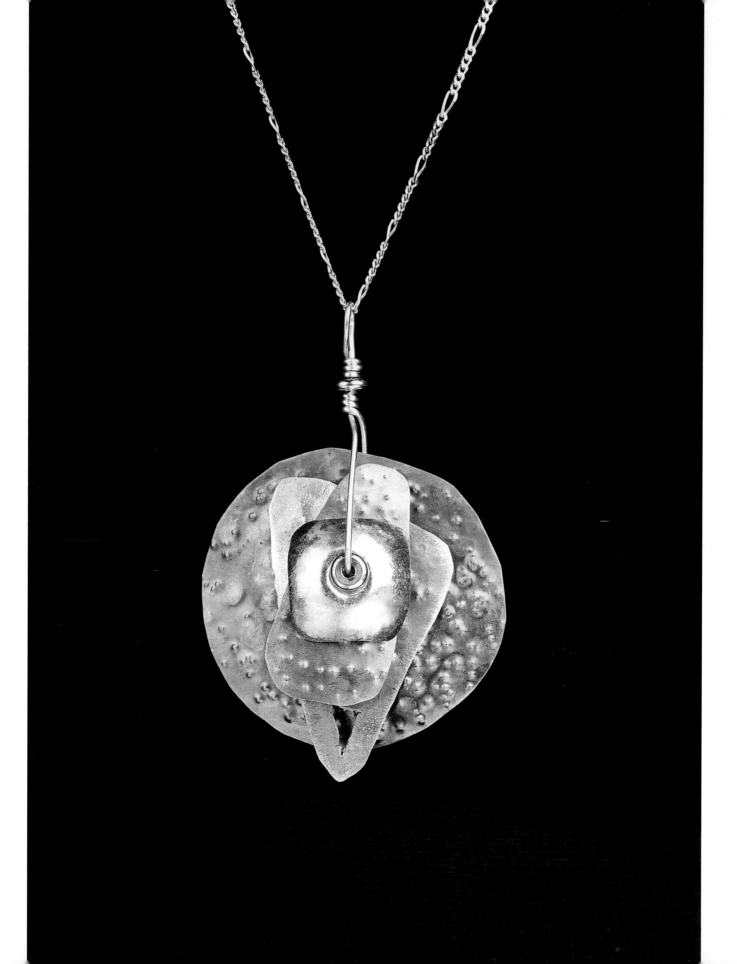

Stacked Spinner Necklace

I chose this project to be first in the book due to its simplicity. The design of the necklace lets you concentrate on learning technique, as it will be correctly made no matter what its dimensions, materials, or style. Have fun, and begin to create!

TECHNIQUES

Cutting and forging sheet metal
Cutting a window in metal sheeting
Texturing
Punching holes
Wire wrapping

MATERIALS

Sheeting:
Brass, 28-gauge, 2 x 3 inches
(5.1 x 7.6 cm)
Silver, 30-gauge, 2 x 2 inches
(5.1 x 5.1 cm)

Wire:
Silver or tin-coated, 18-gauge
6 inches (15.2 cm)

Embellishments:
5 to 7 round, silver disc beads,
¼ inch (0.6 cm) in diameter
Ornamental beads (optional)
24 inches (61 cm) of silver neck
chain with clasp

TOOLS

Metal sheet cutters
Block of scrap wood
Safety glasses
Sharpened flat-head screwdriver
Ball-peen hammer
Anvil
Awl
Dapping block
Metal hole punch tool
Pliers

WHAT YOU DO

1 Begin by deciding the sizes and shapes for the layers in your necklace. For the example shown, use the metal sheet cutters to cut two pieces of brass sheeting, one piece a 2-inch (5.1 cm) circle and the second piece a triangle with rounded corners approximately 1 x 1½ inches (2.5 x 3.8 cm). From the silver sheeting, cut two pieces: an irregular triangle a little smaller than the brass circle and a ¾-inch (1.9 cm) square. If the shapes, materials, and sizes vary in your pieces, that's fine. Try to create irregular and varied shapes, as that will give the piece more dimension and movement.

2 Place the triangular silver piece on a scrap of hardwood. Put on a pair of safety glasses, as you will be removing small pieces of metal. To cut a triangular window in the piece, first put the end

of a sharpened screwdriver where one outside edge of the window will be. Hit the screwdriver's handle with the flat face of a ball-peen hammer to cut into the silver. Reposition the screwdriver in a V shape to make the second side of the triangle (see photo A). Complete the triangle by making a third cut, and remove the inside silver piece.

3 Place the silver triangle on the anvil, and use the ball end of the ball-peen hammer to forge the edges of the window. Continue to forge the edges of all of the silver and brass pieces to create a deckled effect and a smooth texture.

4 Add texture and make patterns to any or all of the pieces by using the awl and hammer to create indentations and bumps (see photo B).

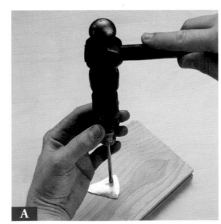

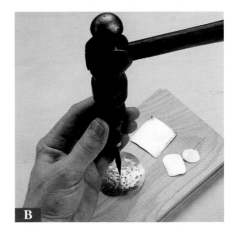

Stacked Spinner Necklace

5 Place the small square of silver on the dapping block. Using the ball end of the hammer, forge the center area of the square (see photo C). If you do not have a dapping block, you can achieve similar results by focusing your hammering on the center area to add a cupped shape to the piece.

6 To decide where the holes will be for the hanger, arrange the pieces in a stacked series. Placing the holes slightly off center creates more visual interest. Mark the chosen spot on each piece of metal by hammering an indentation with the awl.

7 Use a hole punch tool to punch the holes into each metal piece. (See page 25 in the Basics section for more on punching holes.)

8 Take the 6-inch (15.2 cm) piece of silver wire, bend it at one-third of its length with the pliers, and gently hammer the bend to make it work hard.

Thread the long end through one silver washer disc and then through the small, silver square piece of metal (see figure 1). Continue with the other metal pieces, using discs in between each piece.

9 Once all the metal pieces are threaded on the wire, add a last disc and then bend the wire again, leaving approximately ⅛ inch (0.3 cm) extra space on the length of wire that holds all the pieces and discs. Making this hanger shape will allow the pieces to move freely. Make the two sides of the wire cross just above the edge of the largest metal piece, and make a wrapped loop, with the short end of the wire doing the wrap. (See the section on wire loops on page 26 in the Basics section.)

10 Add a washer bead to the top of the wrap (or any other embellishment beads you choose) before you make the final wrapped loop. The final wrapped loop should have a large enough loop to thread the neck chain through.

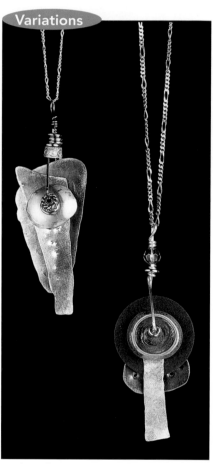

As these alternative pieces show, you will never run out of ideas once you begin to vary the shapes, materials and objects you add to the Stacked Spinner Necklace.

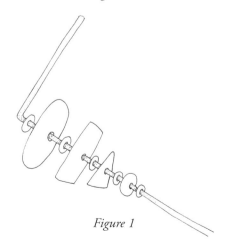

Figure 1

Folded Earrings

The copper sheeting folded into these striking earrings has been given a heat patina.
You can also add texture, colored patinas, or embellishments to achieve a variety of
looks. One great thing about these earrings is that there is no right or wrong side,
which makes them beautiful at any angle.

Folded Earrings

TECHNIQUES

Cutting metal sheeting
Applying heat-treated patinas
Burning balls on and forging
wire ends
Wire wrapping

MATERIALS

Sheeting:
Copper, 18-gauge, 5 x ½ inches
(14 x 1.3 cm)

Wire:
Copper, 24-gauge, 5 feet (1.5 m)
Copper, 18-gauge, 20 inches
(50.8 cm)

Embellishments:
12 small assorted beads
1 pair of silver hook ear wires

TOOLS

Metal sheet cutters
Needle-nose pliers
Torch
Safety glasses
Metal hole punch tool
Wire cutters
Hammer
Anvil
Drill with ⅛-inch (0.3 cm) bit
or an awl

WHAT YOU DO

1 Cut the copper sheeting lengthwise starting at the middle of one ½-inch (1.3 cm) side, giving you two pieces measuring ½ inch x 2½ inches (1.3 x 6.4 cm) each.

2 Holding them in the pliers, heat-treat the pieces of copper sheeting with the torch. Once you have achieved the desired color, make marks on the inside of each piece where the folds will be. You should repeat the same fold combinations within each pair of earrings (though you can vary the folds in different pairs). On the example in the main photo, the first bend is about ¾ inch (1.9 cm) from one end. About ¼ inch (0.6 cm) beyond that, the second bend forms the bottom of the earring. Do the steps on each earring at the same time to maintain consistency.

3 Once you've shaped the earring, make the last fold where the ear wire will connect. At the spot for the last fold, punch a hole in the center

before actually making the fold (see photo A). Make sure the hole is directly on the fold. This is the top of the earring. Wait to make the final fold until you complete the embellishment beads and ear wire connection.

4 Use wire cutters to cut the length of 24-gauge wire into two pieces approximately 2½ feet (75 cm) long for each earring. Burn one end of each piece to create small balls. Set aside.

5 Cut the 20-gauge wire into four equal pieces approximately 5 inches (12.7 cm) each. With the torch, burn two of the ends of the wires to create balls. To make the inside bead embellishment, take the wire with the melted balls on the ends, and thread on the beads, making sure you have the appropriate amount to fit in the triangle space you will create with the final fold.

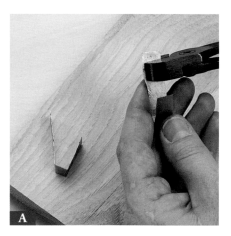

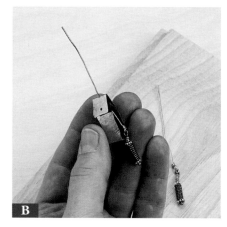

6 Once you've threaded the beads are threaded on the wire, make a wrapped loop at the top of each of the wires.

7 Take the other two remaining lengths of copper wire coming out of the top, and make another wrapped loop to connect the bead embellishment. Thread the wire through the hole, while gently making that final fold as you position everything into place (see photo B). Add some small beads, and finish with a final wrapped loop.

8 Complete the fold by bending the end into its final position. Using the punch, make holes in each of the earrings where the final fold lays over.

9 Take the 24-gauge wire to finish the wire wrap. Thread the balls on each of the earrings through the hole that was just punched. Bring the wire around the side of the earrings in a neat, tight wrap approximately five times on each side of the balls. Secure and finish

the ends of the wire by threading under the wraps or catching the wires within the loops as you wrap the last couple of times (see photo C).

10 For each earring, attach the ear wire to the top of the wrapped loop by gently opening the ear wire and sliding the wrapped loop on it and then closing the ear wire.

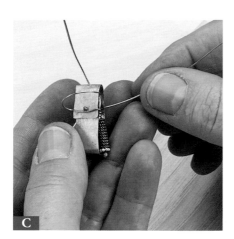

Fold the metals and connect them in a variety of ways to achieve exciting variations.

Bead Shelf Necklace

Making one simple fold can have amazing results when beads are added. This "shelf" necklace showcases your beads in a way that gives them both movement and style. By adjusting the number of sets of beads, lengths or wires, or the size of the copper sheeting, you can alter the look and design of this piece.

WHAT YOU DO

1 Prepare the piece of copper sheeting by cutting halfway into the 2 x 2-inch (5.1 x 5.1 cm) sheet and tapering out to the 2-inch (5.1 cm) length as shown in figure 1.

2 Forge and texture the piece of metal, creating the finish of your choice. (See the section on forging and texturing on pages 38–40 in the Basics section.)

3 Mark with the pen along the edge of the long 2-inch (5.1 cm) side, and punch holes (see photo A) approximately ¼ inch (0.6 cm) apart, starting ¼ inch (0.6 cm) from each end and ⅛ inch (0.3 cm) from the edge (see figure 2). You can instead use a drill with a small bit. Either way, be sure to wear safety glasses.

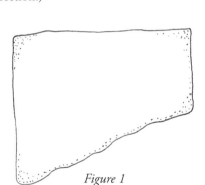

Figure 1

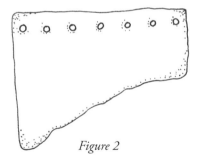

Figure 2

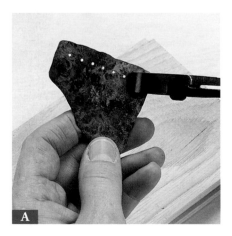

A

Bead Shelf Necklace

You can make your own charms and add more connecting wrapped loops to give this necklace design more movement and personality.

4 Bend the sheeting to create the shelf by either placing it in the vise grip and gently hammering the sheeting over or by bending by hand with a pair of needle-nose pliers (see photo B). Line up the bend approximately ⅛ to ¼ inch (0.3 to 0.6 cm) inside the line of holes.

5 Cut seven pieces of 18-gauge copper wire 4 inches (10.2 cm) long to thread through the holes in your piece. With the propane torch, burn one end of each of the wire pieces to form balls. (See page 34 in the Basics section.)

B

6 Thread the beads on the wires using the balled end to hold them in place. Push the ends of the wires with the beads in place up through the small holes, and decide on the length of each bead dangle. Pull out the two end wires. Cut the wires at the top of the shelf, adjusting the dangles to achieve a variety of total lengths from 1½ to 2 inches (3.8 to 5.1 cm) for each wire. Forge the pieces of wire to create paddles on top of the bead shelf by hammering them on the edge of the anvil with the hammer (see photo C).

7 Take the end dangles, insert them into the end holes, and adjust the length desired for the dangle to hang (see photo D). Take each one out, and lightly hammer just below where the hole in the metal will be on the wire to make that area of the wire thicker.

8 Reinsert the end wires, and make sure they will not pull through the top of the shelf but will instead maintain the desired length. With the remaining length of wire on these end pieces, make a wrapped loop on each piece (see photo E).

9 Finish the necklace by adding the neck chain. With the needle-nose pliers, open up one of the jump rings (see page 31 for information on using jump rings), and thread it through one of the wrapped loops and one end of the chain. Do the same with the other jump ring, wrapped loop, and chain end.

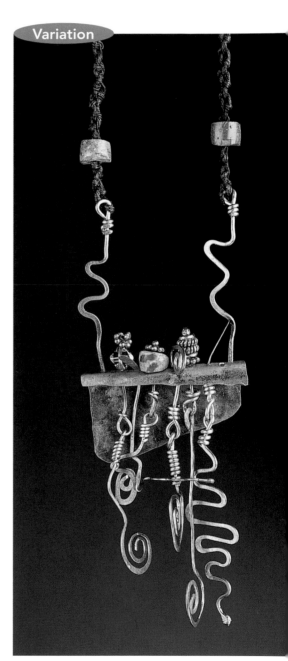

Variation

C

D

E

Layers Necklace

Stitching the elements of this necklace together is the easy part. The hard part is having the time to complete all the ideas you will have from this project. The possibilities are endless, and your creativity will soar as you see how easy and fun it is to connect layers of metals together to make unique and beautiful necklaces.

WHAT YOU DO

1 Begin by preparing the copper and silver sheeting. To make the pictured sample, cut the copper in the tapered shape shown, about ¾ inch (1.9 cm) wide at the widest end. Cut the other end to make a tab in the shape shown about 1 inch (2.5 cm) long. The remaining body of the copper shape will be 2 inches (5.1 cm) tall.

2 Cut the silver sheeting to approximately ½ x 2 inches (1.3 x 5.1 cm). If you want more copper to show around the edges, cut the silver a little smaller.

3 Heat-treat the surface of the silver to patina it and also to anneal it and make it soft.

4 Cut a window in the silver. Place it on the scrap piece of hardwood. Put the end of the sharpened screwdriver where you will cut the outside edge of the window. Hammer the handle end on the sharpened screwdriver to cut into the silver. Gradually move the screwdriver along the area you want cut open to frame the window. Make the complete cut window by connecting the line in a square shape. Remove the inside silver piece after you've completed

Layers Necklace

the window shape. Your window (or series of windows) can be any size you'd like.

5 Forge the edges of the copper and silver pieces to create a deckled effect and a smooth texture. (See page 38 in the Basics section.) Forge the edges on the square of the window to eliminate any sharp edges.

6 Texture and make patterns using the awl and hammer to create indentations and bumps. Insert eyelets in patterns. (For information on how to set eyelets, see page 26 in the Basics section.)

7 Burnish to bring out the shine of the silver and the copper as desired. File, cut, or use a grinder to eliminate any other rough or sharp areas.

8 Connect the necklace by first punching a hole toward the end of the tab, approximately ⅛ to ¼ inch (0.3 to 0.6 cm) from the end (see photo A).

9 Use the pliers to gently bring the tab to the side you want to be the front, gradually rounding the tab with the pliers as you work (see photo B). Place the tab where it will make its final connection.

10 Slide the silver piece under the tab, and mark through the hole on the tab with a small marker. Slide the silver back out, and punch the hole on the mark. Once you've made the tab hole and the silver hole, slide the silver piece back in, and line up the two holes. Punch through both to make the final hole on the piece of copper in the back (see photo C).

11 Take a 2-foot (61 cm) length of 24-gauge copper or silver wire, and burn one of the ends of the wire to create a ball. Thread the ball through a small flat bead and then the tab hole, and then thread it through the silver piece and out the back side of the copper base.

12 Wrap the wire around the entire top area about three times tightly on each side of the bead.

13 End the wrap by sliding the wire in between the copper and the silver sheets and pushing the end against the area that is wrapped to secure it (see photo D). With the pliers, push the area all together from the outside, making sure the end of the wire is not seen through the window that you cut into the silver.

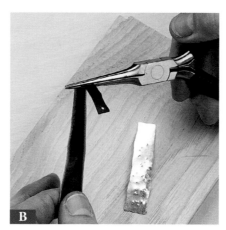

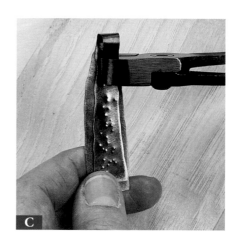

14 Punch a hole to connect the silver and copper bottom pieces together. I usually punch in the center if I am doing just one punch, as this allows the necklace to hang balanced. Thread a 6-inch (15.2 cm) length of wire through the hole, and make a wrapped loop to secure. On the same piece of wire, thread on several beads, and secure the wire by making a wrapped loop. Cut any excess wire off.

15 With the remaining length of wire, burn one of the ends to create a ball. Thread several beads on this wire, making sure that a small bead goes on first to rest in place against the ball. Once the beads are on, thread the other end through the last wrapped loop, and connect this wire with a final wrapped loop. Finish by inserting the neck chain through the holder created by the tab.

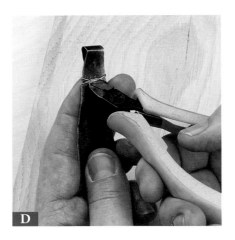

The possibilities are endless in these layered necklaces. Mix the metals, add commercial and handmade charms, and connect them in a variety of ways.

Wrapped Beads Necklace

This necklace, simple in design and shape, is a stunning addition to any outfit. In the version shown here, silver beads peek through the folds of the silver metal sheet, but a different choice of metal and beads could give the piece a very different feel.

TECHNIQUES

Burning balls on wire ends
Bead design
Forging and texturing sheet metal
Applying heat-treated patinas
Wire wrapping

MATERIALS

Sheeting:
Silver, 26-gauge, 3½ x 2 inches
(8.9 x 5 cm)

Wire:
Silver, 18-gauge, 7 inches (17.8 cm)

Embellishments:
8 to 12 beads, assorted sizes and materials
18- to 24-inch (45.7 to 61 cm) silver choker

TOOLS

Torch
Needle-nose pliers
Metal sheet cutters
Awl
Hammer
Anvil
Safety glasses
Round-nose pliers

WHAT YOU DO

1 Hold the 7-inch (17.8 cm) piece of silver wire with pliers, and burn one end with the torch to form a ball. (See page 34–35 in the Basics section.)

2 Decide the length of the wrap by the amount and size of beads you are using. The pictured necklace is about 4 inches (10.2 cm) long, with about 3½ inches (8.9 cm) of beads. Starting with the smallest beads, gradually increase the size as you lay them out in the order you wish them to be positioned in the necklace. Decrease the size of the beads about halfway. Thread the beads on the wire in the order you have established (as shown in photo A).

3 Cut the silver sheet. Make a long, organic, oval shape as also shown in photo A. This shape will allow the pod to have an organic natural opening. The example shown is 4 x 2 inches (10.2 x 5 cm); these dimensions will make a wrap approximately 3¾ inches (9.5 cm) long.

4 Texture with the awl, forge with the hammer, and heat-patina the piece of silver. (See pages 35–40 in the Basics section.)

5 Shape the sheet in a cupped form and gently roll one of the ends with pliers (see photo B). Using the hammer and anvil, gently hammer the piece of metal into a subtly cupped form to hold the beads.

A

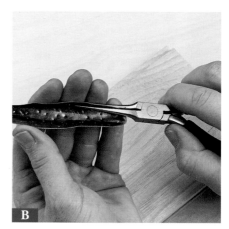

B

Wrapped Beads Necklace

6 Slide the beads into the cone to establish the final length and shape. If more or fewer beads are needed, adjust accordingly. Secure the end of the wire with the ball, and position it outside the pod, allowing all the beads to lie inside. Open the metal around the opening with pliers to expose the beads. Secure the metal around the wire on both ends by crimping the metal around the wire with pliers.

7 Once the beads are in place, make a wrapped loop with the wire at the top of the piece. (See pages 26–28 in the Basics section.) Gently hammer the edges of the silver sheeting to hold the beads in tightly and securely. With needle-nose pliers, fold the edges of the silver sheet back about ⅛ inch (0.3 cm) See photo C. Make sure all rough edges have been secured and the piece is tight and smooth. Thread the wrapped loop in the silver choker.

Variations

Many variations on the pod can be achieved by changing the beads and the way the metal folds around the piece.

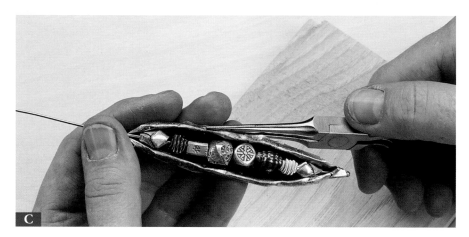

C

CHAPTER 2
Commercial Cold Connections

"Cold connection" is given a whole new meaning in the construction of the following projects. In the jewelry designs in this chapter, an industrial feel takes a front seat. You'll use hardware and commercial items such as rivets, eyelets, nuts, and bolts to assemble and accent the pieces. After making these pieces, you may never look at a nut and bolt the same way again.

Each project in this chapter uses a flat piece of sheet metal cut into a specific shape or series of shapes. As in Chapter 1, most projects require you to apply a heat patina to give the metal an aged look and some variation in color. The first project, a simple pair of earrings made of copper and silver sheeting, gives you a chance to explore the metal products found in scrapbooking and hardware stores. Next, a "window" pin containing a woven grid of a variety of materials as its focal point allows you to learn about weaving.

The watch project that follows takes cold connection items to a decorative level, using small eyelets as decorative circles. The fourth project is a necklace that proves that less can be better. You'll texture one long piece of silver, and then cut tiny windows into it. After gently folding it into shape, you'll finally connect it with a nut and a bolt. The final project is a wonderful bracelet you'll create from a series of silver sheeting squares, patina copper circles, rivets, and jump rings connected together by a chain mail pattern.

All these projects use basic metalsmith techniques, such as heating, cutting, and forging. As with every piece of jewelry in this book, no soldering is required. Creating jewelry with cold-connection techniques makes things easier and faster, leaving you more time to focus on the designs and textures you'll use to create these striking pieces.

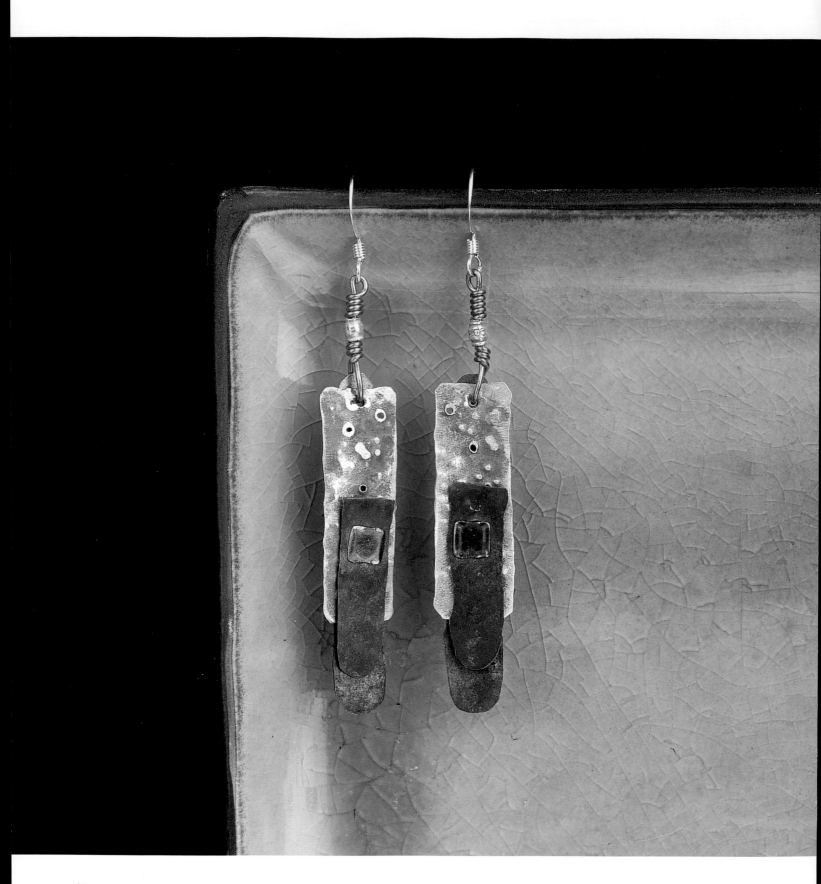

Mixed Metal Earrings

Using brads or eyelets and a few bits of copper and silver, you can make these fun, eclectic earrings in no time at all. I enjoy mixing the metals to achieve a variety of styles and looks.

TECHNIQUES

Applying heat-treated patinas
Using liver of sulphur patina
Installing eyelets and brads
Making wire-wrapped loops

MATERIALS

Sheeting:
Silver, 24-gauge, 1½ x 2 inches
(3.8 x 5.1 cm)
Copper, 18-gauge, 1 x ½ inches
(2.5 x 1.3 cm)

Wire:
Copper or silver, 20-gauge,
6 inches (15.2 cm)

Embellishments:
8 to 12 beads, assorted sizes
and materials
18- to 24-inch (45.7 to 61 cm)
silver choker

TOOLS

Sheet metal cutters
Propane torch
Two pairs of needle-nose or
flat-nose pliers
Hammer
Anvil
Awl
Ball-peen hammer
Metal file
Block of scrap wood
Hole punch tool
Safety glasses
Leather glove

WHAT YOU DO

1 Cut two to four pieces of the silver and the copper sheeting in a variety of shapes, each 1 to 2 inches (2.5 to 5.1 cm) long and ¼ to ½ inch (0.6 to 1.3 cm) wide. Make each shape in a set of two for the pairs of earrings (see photo A).

2 With the torch, heat-treat the silver and copper pieces to patina the surface of the silver and to anneal it and make it soft. Hammer the edges of the copper to make them smooth and create a deckled effect. Texture the surface by using the awl or the ball part of a ball-peen hammer.

3 Place each set of pieces in a design that you like by overlapping the silver and the copper. Use the awl and hammer to make an indentation where the two metals will connect with a brad or eyelet.

4 Punch through the indentations with the hole punch (see photo B). Connect the metals on each earring with an eyelet or brad. (See page 26 in the Basics section.)

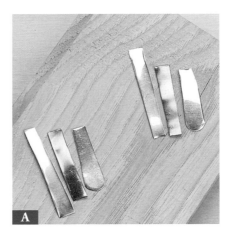

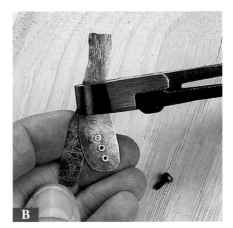

Mixed Metal Earrings

5 Punch small holes at the top center of the earring to attach the ear wires (see photo C). Connect the ear wires by making a wrapped loop on the top of the earring from the hole you punched.

6 Add a small bead to accent and space between the two wrapped loops. Make the second wrapped loop, and make sure that the wrap returns and meets snugly with the bead you added.

7 Open the ear wires as you would a jump ring, separating the circle by sliding it with two pliers to the side. (Opening the circle by pulling it apart can change the circle shape and weaken it.) Loop the ear wire on the wrapped loop. Close the ear wire loop by sliding it back into place gently.

Variations

As you make more earrings using this technique, you can cut interesting shapes and texture the metals in a variety of ways.

C

Woven Windows Pin

For this stylish pin, you weave copper foil and paper together to insert into its window opening. Industrial screws and nuts are used as the cold connection to assemble the piece.

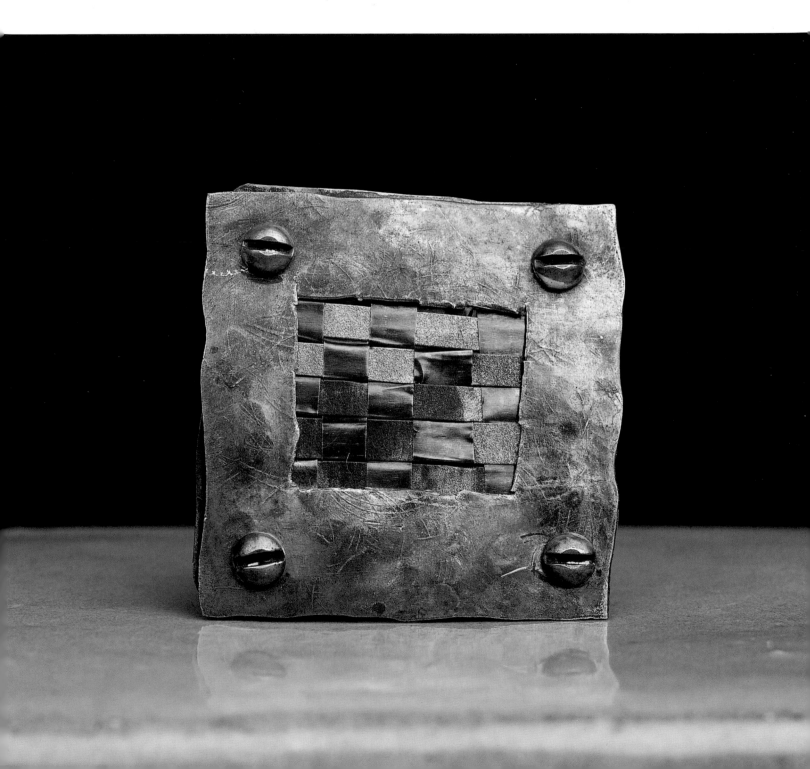

Woven Windows Pin

TECHNIQUES

Cutting windows in metal sheeting
Applying heat-treated patinas on
copper foil
Weaving over/under a grid

MATERIALS

Sheeting:
Copper sheeting, 18-gauge, two
pieces, each 1½ inches (3.8 cm)
square
Copper foil, .002 thickness,
1 x 2 inches (2.5 x 5.1 cm)
Card stock paper, painted with
metallic paints, or printed card
stock

Findings and embellishments:
4 metal or brass nuts and bolts
1 silver bar pin, 2 to 2½ inches (5.1
to 6.4 cm) long

TOOLS

Propane torch
Pliers
Sharpened flat-head screwdriver
Scrap piece of hardwood
Hammer
Anvil
Scissors
Glue
Paper clips or clothespins
Awl
Safety glasses
Drill with ⅛ inch (0.3 cm) bit
Block of scrap wood
Leather glove

WHAT YOU DO

1 Heat-treat two pieces of copper sheeting to patina the surface. Move each piece in and out of the flame to create color, then let them cool.

2 Cut the window by placing one of the treated squares on the scrap piece of hardwood. Place the end of the screwdriver where the outside edge of the window will be. Hammer the handle end on the sharpened screwdriver to cut into the copper. Gradually move the screwdriver along the square area you want cut open for the window. Make the complete cut window by connecting the line in a square shape. Remove the inside copper piece once the cut is completed in the window shape. Your window or series of windows can be any size.

3 With the hammer and anvil, forge the edges on the square of the window. Forge the edges of the copper pieces to create a deckled effect and smooth texture.

4 To make the woven insert for the window, take a piece of copper foil, and treat the surface with the torch using the same technique used for the sheeting. Keep in mind that it is thinner and cannot be left in the flame as long or it will melt. One option is to use the cat food patina, as described on page 38 of the Basics section, on this piece.

5 Cut into one side of the copper foil piece, creating strips approximately ⅛ to ¹⁄₁₆ inches (0.3 to 0.16 cm) in width. Leave the strips connected on the other side (see figure 1).

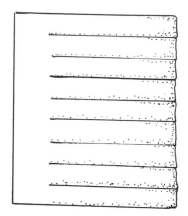

Figure 1

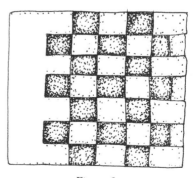

6 Cut the material for weaving into strips approximately the same strip width as the cut foil (see photo A). The length should be a little longer than the copper foil piece so that it will be easier to weave. I use a card stock paper that is either painted with metallic paints or printed with a nice design.

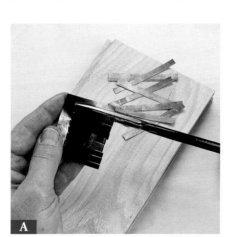

7 Begin the over/under weaving by threading the paper in and out of the copper foil. The foil strips can be positioned in the over/under pattern with the paper laid in if weaving the paper is too difficult. Either way, follow each row with the opposite weave to create the grid (see figure 2).

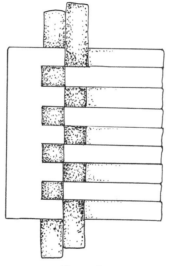

Figure 2

8 End by bending the ends of the copper foil to hold the last row in place. Cut the woven paper ends to the edge of the copper foil. Bend the attached side around to the back if the grid needs to be reduced in size. Cut the paper edge sides to fit in the copper sheeting pieces and to be properly positioned to expose the weaving through the window you have cut (see figure 3).

Figure 3

Woven Windows Pin

9 To better secure the pieces, you can put glue around the windows on the inside of the piece before you sandwich the three pieces together (see photo B). If gluing, hold the layers together with metal clips or clothespins while drying. Make sure that the weaving area does not extend to the corners of the copper sheeting or will not be too large. It just needs to be secured about ⅛ inch (0.3 cm) inside the window.

10 On the back of the back piece of copper, mark two squares where the pin back ends need to be inserted, and cut holes with the screwdriver (see photo C).

11 Put a small amount of glue on the pin back, and insert it into the holes you have created (see photo D). Let it dry.

12 Using the hammer and awl and wearing safety glasses, mark the four corners where you will place the screws. Place the copper piece on a piece of wood, and hammer on the handle of the awl, placing the awl's point where the screws will be.

13 Drill the four holes with a ⅛-inch (0.3 cm) bit. Wear safety glasses, and hold the piece of copper firmly against the scrap wood on a table surface. Secure the copper piece by holding it with the leather glove or using a clamp in order to avoid any injury in case the copper piece slips.

14 Secure the back piece of copper to the front by attaching the small screws and nuts (see photo E).

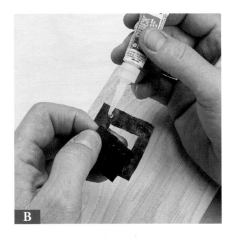

B

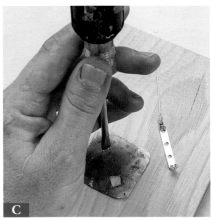

C

D

E

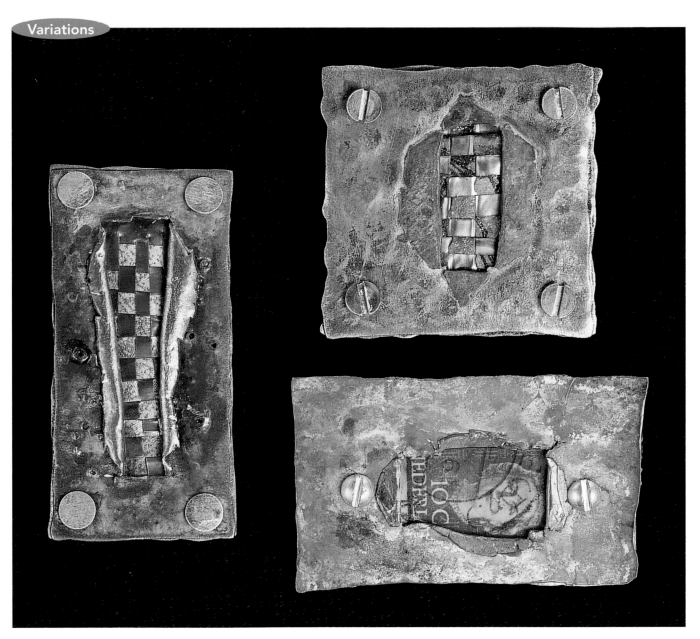

If you make the window pin into a necklace, you can also use the back copper piece to create another window or series of cut-outs, making a reversible piece full of interest on both sides.

Silver Watch Bracelet

With its sleek shapes and simple textures, this contemporary watchband is a real eye-catcher. Small eyelets are used to create a variety of patterns, and jump rings allow you to connect the parts with an easy cold-connection technique.

Applying heat-treated patinas
Using liver of sulphur patina
Installing eyelets

MATERIALS

Sheeting:
Silver, 24-gauge, 2½ x 2½ inches
(6.4 x 6.4 cm)

Findings and embellishments:
Watch face (preferably one with
four round hoops)
35 to 40 small silver eyelets,
1⁄16-inch (0.16 cm) in diameter
32 round silver jump rings,
5 mm and 18-gauge
Claw hook clasp
2 round silver jump rings,
10 mm and 16-gauge

TOOLS

Sheet metal cutters
Propane torch
Pliers
Hammer
Anvil
Silver/black solution
Metal hole punch tool
Safety glasses
Leather glove
Awl
Metal file
Small eyelet tool
Brass brush

WHAT YOU DO

1 Cut six to eight pieces of silver sheeting in sets of two. The pictured project includes two pieces each of ½ x 1 inch (1.3 x 2.5 cm), ¾ x ¾ inch (1.9 x 1.9 cm), and ½ x ¼ inch (1.3 x 0.6 cm).

2 Heat-treat one of each of the sizes of squares to patina the surface, add color to the silver, anneal it, and make it soft.

3 With the hammer and anvil, forge the edges of the silver pieces to create a deckled effect and a smooth texture. Use the silver/black (a hydrochloric acid solution) to darken one of the ¾-inch (1.9 cm) squares.

4 Punch holes in the corners where they will connect with jump rings to assemble (see photo A). Punch a hole in the smallest rectangle on one side to attach a 10 mm jump ring and the claw hook.

5 Punch holes in a random pattern on the two ¾ x ¾-inch (1.9 x 1.9 cm) pieces (see photo B). Punch three

to four holes in a line on the ½ x 1-inch (1.3 x 2.5 cm) pieces. Insert eyelets in the holes, and use the eyelet tool to set.

6 Burnish some of the pieces to bring out a shine on parts of their surfaces.

7 To connect the bracelet together, open jump rings and feed them into the connecting holes on the bracelet. Work in one jump ring at a time to connect the two pieces.

8 Attach one jump ring in between the connecting jump rings to make the watchband lie correctly (see photo C).

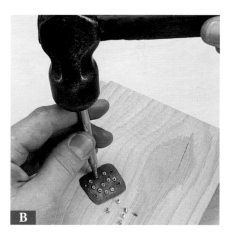

B

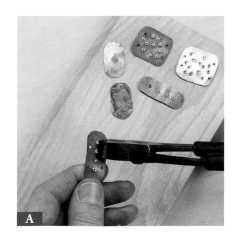

A

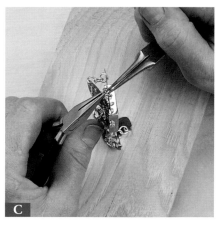

C

Dimensional Necklace

A piece of silver sheeting and a bolt and nut from the hardware store combine to make this industrial-looking necklace. Small windows add a geometric design and accentuate the dimensional quality of the necklace.

WHAT YOU DO

1 Hammer or forge the edges of the silver sheeting piece to create a deckled effect and remove any sharp edges. Dip the piece in a liver of sulphur bath to darken it.

2 Using the sharpened screwdriver, you'll cut four windows down the center of the piece of silver. First, place the silver sheeting on the scrap of hardwood. Start the first window ¾ inch (1.9 cm) from one end of the piece. Hammer the handle end on the sharpened screwdriver to cut into the silver. Gradually move the screwdriver around the area you want cut out. Remove the inside silver piece once the cut is completed in the window shape. Each square will be approximately ⅛ to ¼ inch (0.3 to 0.6 cm) on all sides with about the same space in between each opening.

3 Forge the edges on the cut square of the window. Flip over the silver piece, and place it on the block of scrap wood. Using the awl tapped with the hammer, create patterns of texture on the back side of the piece (see photo A).

4 With the awl and hammer, make a mark about ¼ inch (0.6 cm) from the end of the silver piece that has the windows. Using the ⅛-inch (0.3 cm) drill bit in the hand drill or drill press, drill a hole through this indentation.

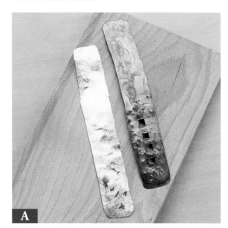

A

Dimensional Necklace

When you use this simple fold design, you can obtain a whole new look by changing the width, the number of windows, and the materials.

5 Burnish the bumps and edges with a burnishing tool or on your anvil by rubbing it on the surface. Measure 2½ inches (6.4 cm) from one end, and mark the piece's middle. Place the needle-nose pliers on the middle mark, and bend both sides up around the pliers to create a small, rounded bottom to the piece (see photo B).

6 Once you've bent the back side to meet the front side, use the awl and hammer (as you did on the first hole) to mark the back side of the piece through the existing ⅛-inch (0.3 cm) hole to know where to drill (see photo C).

7 Drill through the existing hole to drill out the back one. File or use the brass brush on the back nut to finish the piece. Thread the neck chain under the bolt to complete the necklace.

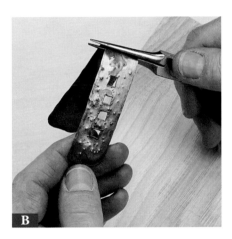

Riveted Chain Mail Bracelet

Using jump rings in a chain mail design as cold connections, along with rivets as embellishments, this simple bracelet is not only a great accent piece but is also very comfortable to wear. I consider this a great "working" bracelet, as it moves easily with your wrist.

TECHNIQUES

Texturing with an awl
Drilling holes
Applyin heat-treated patinas
Using liver of sulphur patina
Installing rivets
Adding jump rings
Making chain mail

MATERIALS

Sheeting:
Silver, 28-gauge, 2 x 2 inches
(5.1 x 5.1 cm) and 3 x 3 inches
(7.6 x 7.6 cm)
Copper, 18-gauge, 2 x 2 inches
(5.1 x 5.1 cm)

Findings and embellishments:
4 standard ⅛-inch (0.3 cm) rivets
115 to 125 silver jump rings,
18-gauge
Silver 3-ring connection slide
clasp, ½ inch (1.3 cm)

TOOLS

Sheet metal cutters
Ball-peen hammer
Anvil
Awl
Safety glasses
Metal hole punch tool
Propane torch
Drill with ⅛ inch (0.3 cm) bit or awl
Liver of sulphur
Brass wire brush or bench polisher
Needle-nose pliers
Round-nose or chain-nose pliers

WHAT YOU DO

1 Cut four square shapes from the silver sheet. Size them as you wish; the squares shown in the project photo are approximately 1 inch (2.5 cm) across. Round out the edges by cutting the corners in a curved shape (see photo A).

2 Forge the squares around the edges. Using the ball side of the hammer, forge each square area, making it cup toward you as you hammer repeatedly in the center of the square.

3 After the square pieces are shaped, texture their surfaces with the awl. Using the small hole punch, punch holes on opposite sides of each square where you will connect the jump rings.

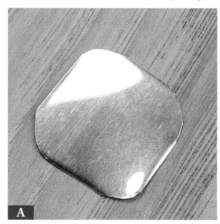

A

4 Make a mark in the center of each square. Drill in the center of the square using the hand drill or drill press and the ⅛-inch bit.

5 Heat-treat the copper sheet to achieve a red patina, using the cold-water patina and propane torch method. (See pages 32–38 in the Basics section.)

6 Mark with the awl the four points in which to drill holes for the circles you will cut. (Because the copper circles are so small once cut, it is much easier and safer to do this now while the sheet is still intact). Drill the four holes in the sheeting with the ⅛-inch (0.3 cm) drill bit.

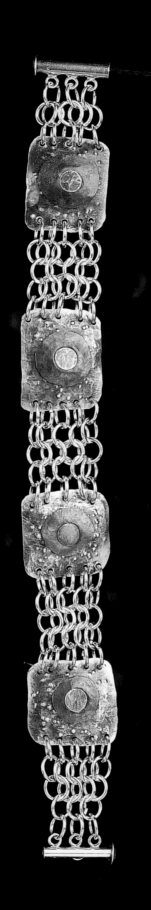

Riveted Chain Mail Bracelet

7 Cut small circles with the metal cutters around the drilled holes (see photo B). Make sure their size is appropriate for the area between the holes punched for the jump rings. Also, make the circles large enough to be seen after you place the rivet. I prefer the circles not be totally even, so I just eyeball their circumference. However, if you prefer a more symmetrical shape, you can mark where you will cut.

8 Lightly hammer the circles to achieve a slight domed effect. Do not hammer too hard, or you will lose the shape of your drilled hole. If a hole is not even after lightly hammering, you can open and even it up again by using the awl.

9 Dip the silver square in the liver of sulphur solution. Gently polish off the tops of the bumps and the edges of the squares with the brass brush or polisher to create your desired effect. Use four rivets to connect the circle piece to the square sheeting for each section.

10 As shown on the sample squares, place jump rings in five holes on two opposite sides of each square. Use small sections of a chain mail technique to assemble the bracelet. Lay the sections in the order you wish them to be placed.

11 Open the jump rings by sliding them side to side with the two pliers to maintain their circular shape (see photo C). Insert five jump rings into the five drilled holes, and close them by slowly sliding the jump ring just past the final closed position then gently moving it back into the closed position. Put a small amount of pushing pressure on the ring, so the connection is tight and has no gaps.

12 Figure 1 shows the pattern to follow for adding the other jump rings. Connect each of the four squares with this pattern.

13 To connect the two parts of the slide clasp to each end of the bracelet, follow the diagram and pattern of connection of the jump rings.

B

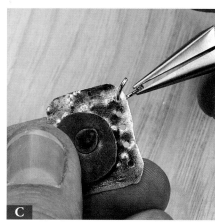
C

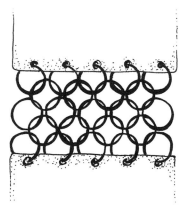
Figure 1

CHAPTER 3
Wire Work

I began my art career with weaving. When I expanded my work into jewelry, I translated a woven quality into the jewelry I designed. I found early on that basket-weaving techniques interpreted well into jewelry designs. Because of my background, I tend to explore connections with ties, stitches, and weaves while avoiding the soldering techniques used by other metalsmiths. The five projects in this chapter allow you to experiment with several weaving techniques.

The first project uses the sumac stitch, a weave generally used in loom weaving that offers a technique you can take to other projects. The next project incorporates knotless netting, also known as the blanket stitch in sewing, or as looping in basketry. The third project is a wire bracelet that is the most free-form piece in the book. Tackle it correctly on the technical level, but don't forget to have fun creatively.

The fourth project in this chapter, a cone-shaped necklace, uses a twining technique, along with some of the wrapping skills learned in Chapter 1. The last project combines copper wire, beads, and fishing swivels with twining to make what is probably the most fun and whimsical piece in the book.

The projects in this section are some of my favorites. Using weaving techniques will open up new possibilities in making jewelry for you, just as it did for me. As you work through the projects, consider taking one technique and applying it to a new shape or another project design. You can (and should) interchange the elements from all of these projects to create new and innovative possibilities.

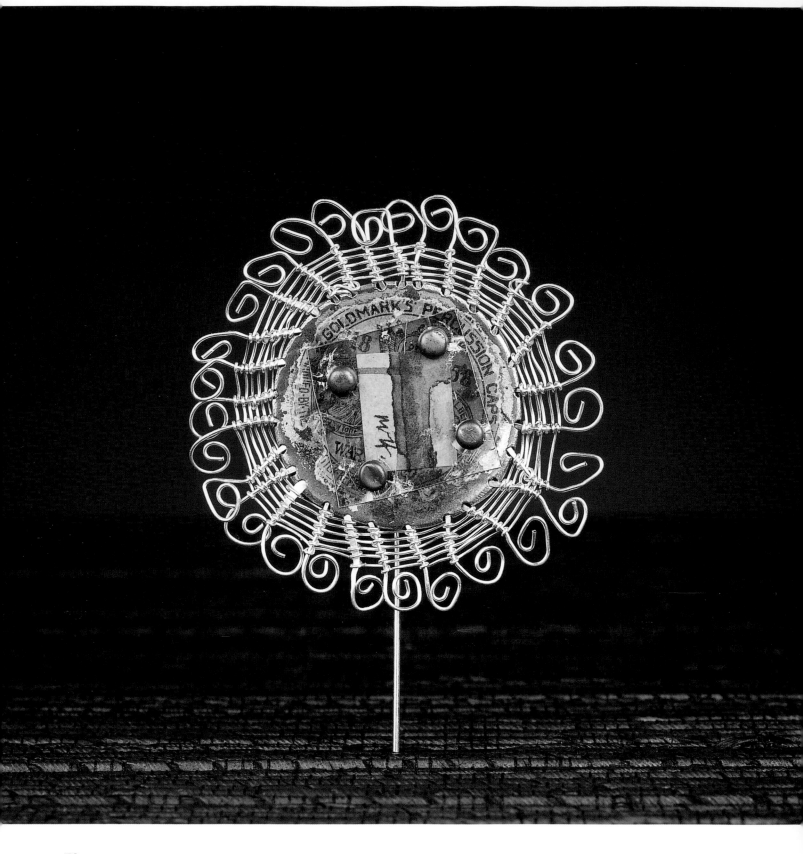

Tin Lid Pin

Using antique metal and tin lids—you can also use bottle caps—as the center of a piece of jewelry is an entirely new way of recycling. This easy wrapped-wire project will have everyone taking a second look.

TECHNIQUES

Forging wire
Doing a sumac weave
Making wire-wrapped loops

MATERIALS

Wire:
Silver, 18-gauge, 30 inches (75 cm)
Craft wire, 26- or 24-gauge, 6 feet (1.8 m)

Findings and embellishments:
Tin lid or bottle cap
Small picture or paper image
Piece of mica, approximately 1 inch (2.5 cm) square
4 small brads
Silver neck chain, 18 to 24 inches (45.7 to 61 cm)

TOOLS

Drill with ⅛-inch (0.3 cm) bit
Awl (optional)
Safety glasses
Scissors
Hammer
Anvil
Needle-nose pliers

WHAT YOU DO

1 Drill (or poke with the awl) holes in the top of the rim of the tin lid or bottle cap. Make the holes as close to the edge as possible, and leave about ⅛ inch (0.3 cm) of space between each hole (see photo A). The tin lid in this main photo is 1½ inches (3.8 cm) in diameter, which requires about 28 to 30 holes. A bottle cap, which is about 1 inch (2.5 cm) across, needs about 18 to 20 holes. Sand the rough edge of the new-formed holes.

2 Decorate the surface of the lid by cutting the small picture, watercolor, image, or paper to fit on the lid. Cut the small piece of mica to cover the image. With the ⅛-inch (0.3 cm) bit, drill four holes through the lid at the four corners of the mica and paper. Secure the mica and image to the lid using the brads, as shown in the middle piece in photo B.

3 For each hole in the tin lid or bottle cap, cut a 3-inch (7.6 cm) piece of silver wire. Also cut one piece 8 inches (20.3 cm) in length. With the hammer and anvil, forge just one end on each of the wire pieces.

A

B

Tin Lid Pin

4 Next, put one spoke in each drilled hole, with the 8-inch (20.3 cm) spoke in one hole and the 3-inch (7.6 cm) ones in the rest. The unforged ends should go in through the back of the circle piece. Pull them through to leave the forged ends snug against the holes (see photo C).

5 Cut a 6-foot (1.8 m) length of craft wire. Start the sumac wrap by letting the spoke hang down, and thread the wire around the long spoke.

C

Do an easy wrap by going behind two spokes then looping over the front of the second and going behind the next spoke. Loop over it again in the same manner (see figure 1).

6 Wrap each spoke the same way around the entire circle. When you reach the long spoke again, keep wrapping. On this row, start to bend the spokes back so they lie flat (see photo D). It may take a couple rows to completely get them flat. The forged ends will lie flat inside the cup of the lid area. Once the spokes are flat, leave the ends straight out to curl later.

7 Continue to do the sumac stitch until you reach a desired diameter. Finish the stitch by tucking the end wire back through the stitch in the row before where you began the weave. Secure it around the long top spoke.

8 Cut a circle to fit inside the back of the lid. The circle may be of any material that fits: metal, felt, canvas, card stock paper, leather, or found object (see photo E). Secure it over the pounded wire ends.

9 Hammer down the rim of the pop lid to hold the circle in place, working very slowly and gently to make the circle even. If using a tin lid, cut it every ¼ inch (0.6 cm) or less to have it lie one over the other as it folds flat.

10 You can curl the wire on the ends if you wish, or you can leave them straight. Hammer gently to secure and make the wire work hard, as shown in figure 2.

11 Hammering the ends of the wire or folding the spokes to the back (see figure 3) are just a couple of the alternative methods you can use for finishing the spokes.

Figure 1

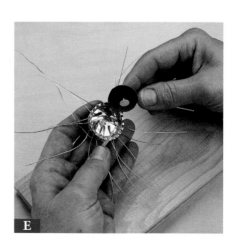

E

Using a smaller gauge wire on these pieces can make it more difficult to weave, but once you try it you will love the detail the smaller wire gives the finished pin.

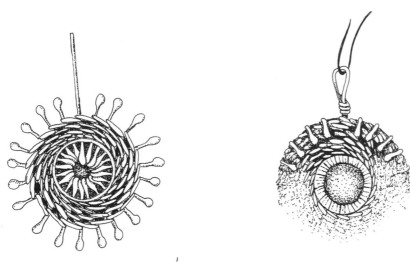

Figure 2

Figure 3

Looped Silver Cone Necklace

In sewing, the type of stitching used on the surface of this piece is known as the buttonhole stitch. In basketry it is called knotless netting, while many fiber artists refer to it as looping or the half hitch. Whatever name you use, this is one of those universal stitches that can lead to an amazing number of creative applications.

TECHNIQUES

Applying heat-treated patinas
Forging metal surfaces
Using liver of sulphur patina
Burning balls on wire ends
Creating knotless netting
Making wire-wrapped loops

MATERIALS

Sheeting:
Silver, 28-gauge, at least 2½ inches (6.4 cm) square

Wire:
Copper, 22-gauge, 3½ to 4 feet (105 to 120 cm)
Silver, 18-gauge, 6 inches (15.2 cm)
Silver, 26-gauge, 5 to 7 feet (150 to 210 cm)

Findings and embellishments:
Silver neck chain
1 silver bead

TOOLS

Metal tin snips or cutters
Hammer
Anvil
Liver of sulphur
Burnishing tool
Needle-nose pliers
Wire cutters
Propane torch
Brass brush or bench polisher
Safety glasses
Leather glove

WHAT YOU DO

1 Cut one 28-gauge piece of silver sheeting into a triangle, approximately 2½ inches (6.4 cm) long and 1½ inches (3.8 cm) at the base. The triangle does not need to be totally even. More "organic" triangle shapes work as well as perfectly measured ones.

2 With the hammer and anvil, forge the edges of the triangle to create a deckled effect and a smooth texture. Then dip it into a liver of sulphur bath to create a dark patina.

3 Continue by hammering the surface gently. Burnish the edges to bring back the silver surface and leave the majority of the piece a dark patina. You can add texture to the surface with the awl and hammer, but on this piece I prefer the smooth surface with the edges highlighted by the burnishing tool.

4 Using the long needle-nose pliers, roll the triangle, starting with the top point of the triangle (see photo A). Rolling it tightly will give you a solid cone shape, but if you leave an open gap as you roll, you will later be able to see the strands of wire and the line of the opening.

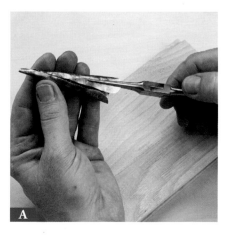

A

Looped Silver Cone Necklace

5 Cut approximately five to seven lengths of copper wire. Their lengths will depend on the individual silver piece you have rolled and the amount of wire fringe you would like hanging out of the bottom. Leave no more than ½ to 1 inch (1.3 to 2.5 cm) hanging out in order to keep wires from bending or getting caught on clothing. Six inches (15.2 cm) of wire length is usually about right. With the torch, burn the ends of the wire to create balls on the ends. Then bend the pieces in half. Thread an 18-gauge piece of silver wire around the centers of the wires, and do a wrapped loop to secure the bundle (see photo B).

6 Prepare for the knotless netting by taking the length of 26-gauge silver wire and cutting it in half to make it more manageable. Take this piece, and secure it by looping it around one or more strands of the wire fringe at the top where it will not show through the gap (see photo C). As you pull the end of the 18-gauge wire through the top of the cone for the hanger, the 26-gauge wire should be alongside of it at the same time (see photo D).

7 Once the 18-gauge wire is in place and the fringe wires are tight and in position, add the bead to embellish before you make a final wrapped loop for the hanger.

8 After the cone is basically complete, begin the surface stitching. The 26-gauge wire now coming out of the top of the cone is secure. Use this as the stitching material. Wrap this length of wire around the outside of the top of the cone in one small circle. This first loop starts the process of looping on, and you build from there. Catch the beginning of the loop as shown to secure it. See figure 1 for the steps to begin the stitching.

9 Begin to loop by threading the end of the wire stitch over the back side of the wire, as you pull around to the front catch the loop in the stitch. Repeat this process along the wire until you have completed the initial circle. Make small stitches, but make sure they have a distinct loop with a visual opening (see figure 2). If you made the stitch too tight, you will not be able to build on them with more stitches.

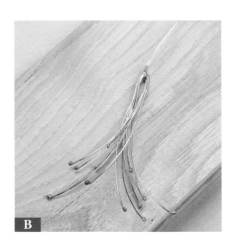

B

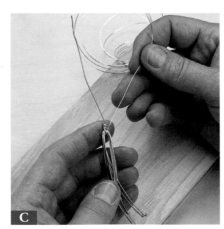

C

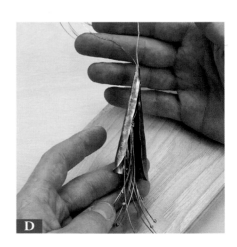

D

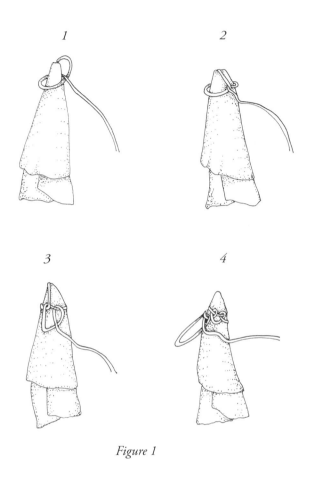

1

2

3

4

Figure 1

Figure 2

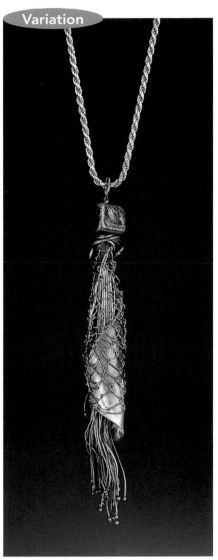

Use sheet metal and wires that are different to create more dimensional pieces and accentuate the looping stitch.

Looped Silver Cone Necklace

10 After you have completed the first row of loops, begin the second row by stitching into an existing loop in the first row (see photo E). This will create the same number of loops as you initially made in the first row. As the cone gradually increases in diameter, you may increase the size of each loop and continue with the same number throughout the piece or increase the number of loops as you proceed. By increasing the number of loops, the loop size remains small and detailed. To increase the number of loops, stitch into an existing row of loops two times. Since the cone's diameter increase is so gradual, do this process on a random basis and probably no more than one time in any given row.

11 Do not let the length of wire get shorter than about 6 inches (15.2 cm), or it will become difficult to add in. When you begin to run out of wire, replace the old wire by inserting the new wire into the last loop made, and carry both wires through a series of a couple of loops. Cut the old short wire flush, and continue with the new piece.

12 When you have reached the bottom of the cone, stitch back into the existing loops, wrapping very tightly, then cut the end.

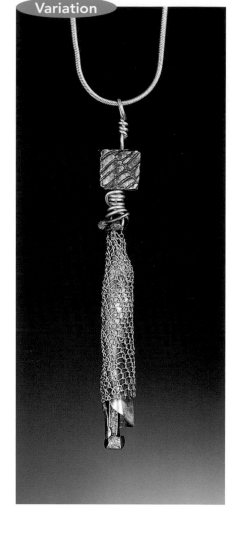

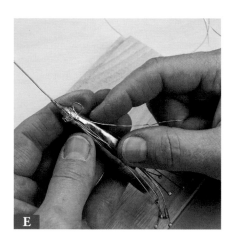

Free-Form Woven Bracelet

The simplest part of this project is the materials list: just some copper wire with beads as a possible addition. The technique is easy, too, but the decisions you need to make with a free-form design make this project a stretch for some people. Try not to over-think this one. Go with the twists, and let the material take you where it will.

Free-Form Woven Bracelet

TECHNIQUES

Wire-wrapping

Over/under weaving with wire

Burning balls on wire ends

MATERIALS

Wire:

Copper, 18-gauge, 5 feet (1.5 m)

Copper, 24-gauge, 25 to 35 feet (8 to 10 m)

Findings and embellishments:

Stone beads (optional)

TOOLS

Propane torch

Hammer

Anvil

Safety glasses

Bracelet mandrel (optional)

Wire cutters

WHAT YOU DO

1 Take the 5-foot (1.5 m) length of 18-gauge copper wire, and burn a ball on each end of the piece.

2 Find the center of the length, and make a circle around your wrist to measure the circumference of your bracelet. Adjust that circle for fit by sliding it over your hand several times. Keep circling your wrist, following the same circumference. If you have a bracelet mandrel, slide the wire on the tool and wrap with the remaining length around it, varying the width that you wrap. If you do not have a mandrel, you can continue to wrap the remaining length around your wrist, constantly checking the circumference to avoid getting too tight or loose. You'll end up with a coil as shown in photo A.

3 Once the bracelet core is established, cut 5 feet (1.5 m) of the 24-gauge wire. Starting in the center of the length of wire, wrap the wire around one or two of the bracelet wires. Take each individual length, and begin weaving using an over-under weave through the larger-gauge wire (see figure 1). Continue this pattern of weaving along the wires (see figure 2).

4 Begin to separate the core wires and, as you do, weave under and over in the area you are separating (see photo B).

5 If an area becomes too tight, or you want to create more visual interest, you can cut the core 18-gauge wire and burn balls on the ends.

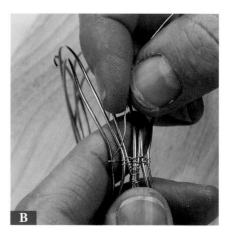

6 As you come to wire that is over-lapping, you can wrap those areas together, creating texture and interest. Continue to weave in and out of the spokes. Be sure to reassess the bigger picture, and constantly look at where you will be headed next in the bracelet. Fill in as much as you want. Add more wire the same way. Finish by cutting the weaver and securing it around the large wire with a couple of wraps.

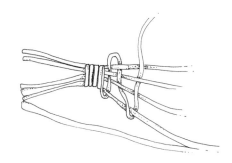

Figure 1

7 As an option: You can add beads to the 24-gauge wire by threading the beads onto the wire (see photo C). Smaller or larger beads can fill in spaces in place of weaving. Remember that sometimes less is better, so plan where to place the beads and how to make them a part of the overall design.

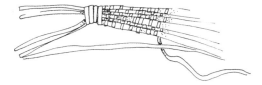

Figure 2

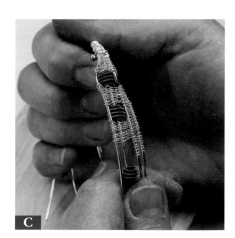

C

Twined Cone Necklace

The techniques used in this project are really a combination of those from two other designs in this chapter. The base is similar to the cone shape in the Looped Silver Cone Necklace, while the twining method is like that used in the Wire-Wrapped Hands Bracelet. This combination of techniques results in a sophisticated necklace.

TECHNIQUES

Forging and texturing sheet metal
Applying heat-treated patinas
Using liver of sulphur patina
Twining
Burning balls on wire ends

MATERIALS

Sheeting:
Silver, 28-gauge, 1 x 2¾ inches
(2.5 x 7 cm)

Wire:
Silver, 20-gauge, approximately
3 feet (90 cm)
Silver, 26-gauge soft, 5 feet
(1.5 cm)

Findings and embellishments:
Silver chain with clasp,
20 to 24 inches (50.8 x 61 cm)

TOOLS

Metal sheet cutters
Propane torch
Hammer
Anvil
Awl
Safety glasses
Liver of sulphur
Metal file
Brass brush
Metal hole punch
Leather glove
Pliers

WHAT YOU DO

1 Cut the 28-gauge silver sheeting into a triangle shape measuring approximately 1 x 2¾ x 2¾ inches (2.5 x 7 x 7 cm). Hammer the edges, and forge and texture the sheet with the awl to obtain an organic shape with interesting deckled edges and bumps, dots, and small holes.

2 Use a bath of liver of sulphur to dip the silver into, and repeat the process of texturing on just the front side of the cone. Burnish this side and its lumps, edges, and high points to bring back the shine of the silver. The opposite side will remain a dark patina from the liver of sulphur.

3 Punch holes with the punch tool, approximately ¹⁄₁₆ inch (0.16 cm) from the edge on the short side (see photo A). Punch as many holes as will fit in the space with approximately ¹⁄₁₆ inch (0.16 cm) in between each hole.

4 Shape the cone by using the pliers to roll the two corners of the 1-inch (2.5 cm) side in to meet (see photo B). Gradually pull and roll toward the long end of the triangle to create a cavern opening. Since the back side's surface remained a dark patina, its contrast when rolled to the front is more dramatic.

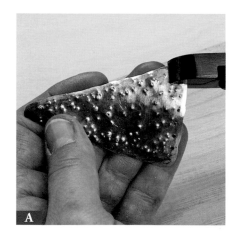

Twined Cone Necklace

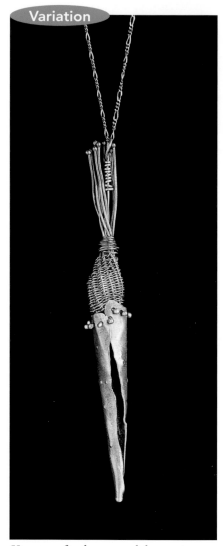

Use copper for the cone and the weaving to achieve a very different look.

5 From the 20-gauge wire, cut one wire 5 inches (12.7 cm) in length (for hanger wire) and the rest in 3-inch (7.6 cm) pieces. The number of 3-inch (7.6 cm) pieces you cut should be the same number as the holes you punched in the triangle. These wire pieces will become the spokes that you will twine around. With the torch, burn one of the ends on each of the wires to create a ball.

6 Insert the spokes into the holes on the cone, leaving the balls to the outside on the top of the cone (see photo C).

7 Take the 5 feet (1.5 cm) of 26-gauge wire, and loop it in half. Take the halfway point and loop it over one of the spokes (see figure 1).

8 Twine as directed in the Wire-Wrapped Hands Bracelet on page 94. However, for this project, continue to twine in a circle around the top of the cone instead of twining flat (see figure 2).

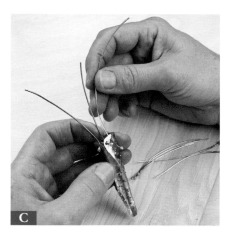

C

9 Continue to build row upon row (see photo D). Put your finger inside and behind as you are twining to hold and secure the spokes. Your finger also is a good mold to help size the piece and give it volume.

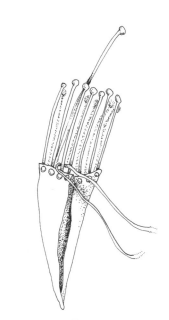

Figure 1

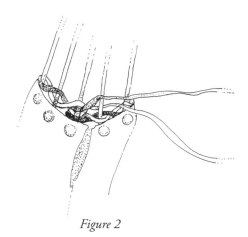

Figure 2

10 The weaving amount is up to you, but 1 inch (2.5 cm) is usually the maximum amount I do. When you are getting ready to end, take your finger out of the weaving, and begin to pull the spokes closer together as you twine (see photo E). Once the weaving becomes more difficult for a row or two and you notice the twining is starting to slip up on the spokes, simply finish by taking both lengths of the weaver and wrapping them tightly around all the spokes several times. Tuck the ends to the inside of the spokes.

11 Do not cut the longer spoke, but push it to the side. Cut the ends of the short wires at the top so they are approximately ½ inch (1.3 cm) long. Burn their ends to create balls.

12 While the long wire is to the side, make a wrapped loop for the necklace to be hung, cutting any excess wire left over from the hanger wire (see photo F).

13 To finish, thread the neck chain through the wrapped loop.

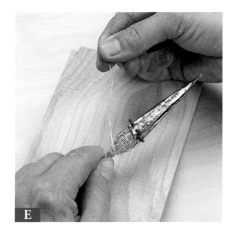

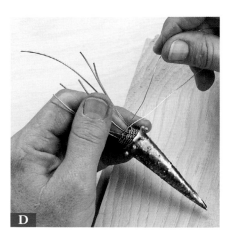

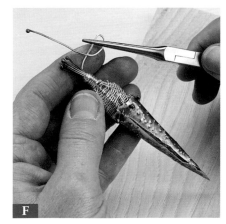

Wire-Wrapped Hands Bracelet

Out of all the projects in this book, this is the one that will really catch everyone's attention. Bend the hands into sign-language letters, and it becomes a very personal symbol of communication.

TECHNIQUES

Burning balls on wire ends
Twining
Wire-wrapped loops

MATERIALS

Wire:
Copper, 18-gauge, 9 feet (2.7 m)
Copper, 24-gauge, 100 feet (30 m)

Findings and embellishments:
32 copper head pins, 24- or 20-gauge 2 to 3 inches
(5.1 to 7.6 cm) long
A variety of approximately 100 small beads (glass, seed, crystal, cut glass, and others)
16 fishing swivels, size 14
Silver or copper toggle and bar clasp

TOOLS

Wire cutters
Propane torch
Pliers
Hammer
Anvil
Safety glasses
Leather glove
Ring holder

WHAT YOU DO

1 Cut 80 pieces of 18-gauge copper wire for the spokes, each ranging in size from ½ to 1¼ inches (1.3 to 3.2 cm). This number will make sixteen hands. With the torch, burn both ends of the wires to create balls.

2 Lay out the spokes in groups of five arranged by the length of fingers (see photo A).

3 Cut a 40-inch (100 cm) length of 24-gauge copper wire to use as the weaver for the spokes. Bend the length in half. Starting with the thumb wire, which will I refer to as a spoke, loop the half length around the thumb spoke as shown in figure 1. You now have two weavers, and you are beginning at the bottom part or wrist area of each hand.

4 To start twining, carry the weaver coming from the back side of the spoke to the next spoke around the back, which in this case is the index finger (see figure 2).

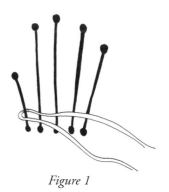

Figure 1

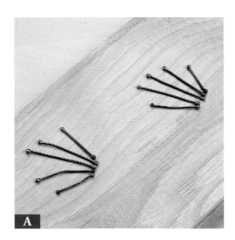

A

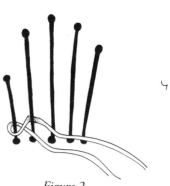

Figure 2

Wire-Wrapped Hands Bracelet

By using colored wire for the twining on the hands, the bracelet can take on a whole new look.

5 Keep adding spokes (fingers in their order) until you reach the pinky finger (see figure 3).

6 Turn the hand to the back side, and continue to twine (see figure 4). If you are right-handed, work to the right, turning the hands at the end to continue in the same direction. Work in the opposite direction if you are left-handed.

Figure 3

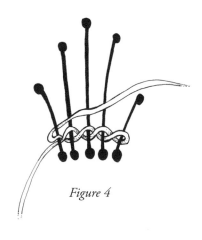

Figure 4

7 Once you have a couple of rows done, place the bottom of the hand where you have been working in the ring holder and secure (see photo B). This will allow you to work easier and not lose your place. Weave the solid bottom area to become the palm of the hand.

8 Once you have reached the point where the thumb exits the palm (look at your own hand) with one of the weavers (see photo C), lay it along the thumb spoke at the end part of the thumbnail area. Continue by wrapping tightly to cover the thumb and the wire by wrapping tightly and solidly back to the thumb base (see figure 5).

9 Continue to twine the palm of the hand (see photo C). For each finger thereafter, starting with the pinky and finishing with the middle finger, follow the same technique of wrapping each digit.

10 After you have completed one hand (see photo D), twine 15 more hands, giving you a total of 16 hands for the bracelet.

11 Cut 16 pieces of 18-gauge copper wire, each about 2 inches (5.1 cm) in length. Using one piece per hand, thread one end into the base of the hand next to the middle finger. (I usually pick the easiest side to insert.) Make a wrapped loop to connect the hand to the piece of wire. Make a wrapped loop on the other end of the wire, wrapping back toward the hand end and securing up next to the initial wrapped area (see figure 6).

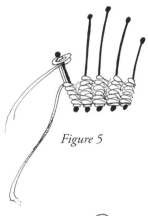

Figure 5

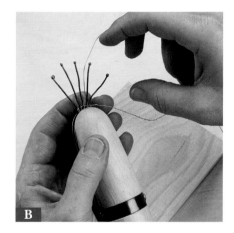

B

Figure 6

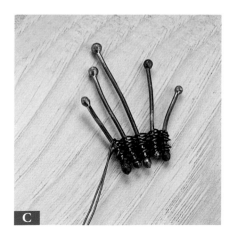

C

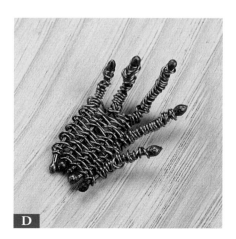

D

Wire-Wrapped Hands Bracelet

12 Using the variety of small crystal, seed, round, and glass beads, thread the beads onto the copper head pins, and secure with a wrapped loop at the top of the head pin.

13 Lay out the bracelet how it will be assembled. I used one hand and two head pins with beads to each fishing swivel in the project in the main photo. The fishing swivels are a lot like safety pins in mechanics. Open the fishing swivel, and thread one wrapped loop of the first hand on the swivel. Then proceed by sliding the bar end of the clasp on, and finish with one head pin before closing the swivel (see figure 7).

14 Open the next fishing swivel. Alternate by threading on two beaded head pins first, followed by hooking this swivel into the back side of the first swivel and ending with threading on the second hand before closing. Each fishing swivel has a small dangle out the back side of it. Leave that hanging. Always hook into the big hole in the back part of the swivel. Alternate back and forth with the hands and bangles into the swivels (see figure 8). It balances the bracelet better.

15 Using 16 swivel connections will create a bracelet to fit most wrists. Adjust if you need to by using more or less. When you reach the last connection swivel, again thread on a hand then the toggle part and only one bead bangle.

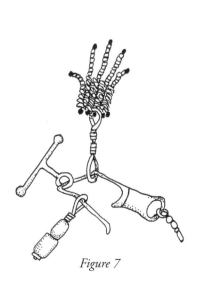

Figure 7

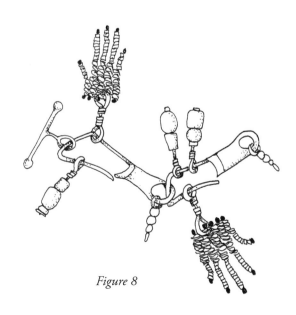

Figure 8

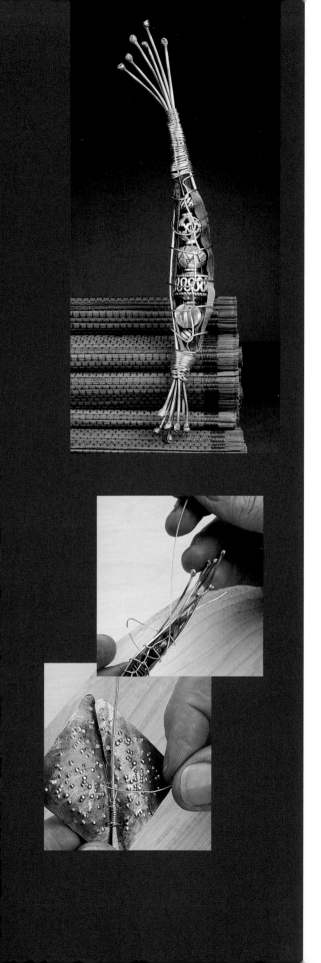

CHAPTER 4
Stitching

The projects in this chapter explore some of the more basic techniques you'll need for working with wire. I love what wire can do and how it makes and enhances connections, both structurally and as decorative accents.

In the earrings of the first project, brass sheeting and silver wire make for a silver and gold combination that I really love; this piece will surely give you many more ideas to build other forms of jewelry. The bracelet in the second project uses the wrapped loop to make its connections. The more wrapped loops you use to connect the copper pieces, the "softer" the bracelet will appear.

The third project—inspired by Japanese packaging methods, of all things—uses silver wire and mesh to capture a line of beads. The fourth project takes a simple concept to achieve stunning results. Two pieces of silver are connected together into a pin using a piece of wire in a technique that gives the illusion of a hinge. This piece has the eerie ability to seem both very industrial and very natural, as if it were both a piece of hardware and an ancient fossil.

In the last project in this chapter (and the last in the book), wire is the star. Delicate wires are twisted to create a branch or tendril effect, with small beads added for visual interest. This twisting method allows you to create any kind of jewelry—bracelets, earrings, a choker, or whatever you'd like.

Moving Parts Necklace and Earrings

Suspended beads and other moving parts make this earring and necklace set fun to make and wear. Using silver beads to embellish it, you'll find that this open-concept jewelry is a breeze to put together in no time at all. Try it in copper to achieve a whole different look.

TECHNIQUES

Applying heat-treated patinas
Burning balls on wire ends

MATERIALS

Sheeting:
Silver, 20-gauge, ⅜ x 5 inches
(1 x 12.7 cm)
Silver, 18-gauge, ½ x 3½ inches
(1.3 x 8.9 cm)

Wire:
Silver, 18-gauge, 12 to 15 inches
(30.5 to 38.1 cm)

Findings and embellishments:
12 to 16 silver beads in various
sizes
Silver neck chain with clasp,
20 inches (50.8 cm)
2 silver ear wires

TOOLS

Sheet metal cutters
Propane torch
Pliers
Hammer
Anvil
Brass brush
Awl
Safety glasses
Wire cutters
Metal hole punch tool

WHAT YOU DO

1 For the earrings, cut two pieces of 20-gauge silver sheeting that are ⅜ x 2 inches (1 x 5.1 cm) each and have rounded corners. For the necklace piece, cut a piece of 18-gauge silver sheeting that is ½ x 3½ inches (1.3 x 8.9 cm), also with rounded corners.

2 Forge the square edges of the silver pieces to create a deckled effect and a smooth texture (see photo A). Use the brass brush to create a smooth matte finish.

3 Find the center points of the silver pieces. Using the hammer and awl, mark a spot on the two earring pieces ⅛ inch (0.3 cm) away from that center toward one end; on the necklace piece, mark a spot ¼ inch (0.6 cm) from that center. This will ensure that the two sides in each piece will not be identical. Punch the holes out with the hole punch (see photo B).

4 On the necklace piece, measure from each side of the center hole to mark holes with the awl at ¾ inch (1.9 cm), 1 inch (2.5 cm), and 1¼ inches (3.2 cm) away. Punch the holes. The other end of the piece should have a matching set of three holes.

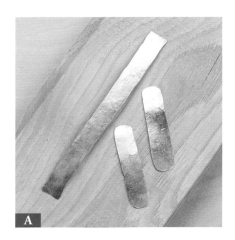

A

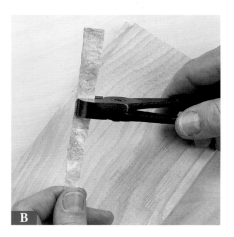

B

Moving Parts Necklace and Earrings

5 On the earring pieces, measure ½ inch (1.3 cm) from the center hole toward both ends of each piece, and mark with the awl. Punch the holes. Punch one hole in a matching position on the other end of the earring piece.

6 Bend the silver necklace piece ½ inch (1.3 cm) from the center on each side at a 90° angle. The three holes on each side should line up perfectly (see photo C).

7 In a similar way, bend the earrings at ¼ inch (0.6 cm) on each side of the center to obtain a width of ½ inch (1.3 cm) at the top. The single holes on each side of the earrings should also line up after bending.

8 For the necklace, cut three 1½-inch (3.8 cm) pieces of the 18-gauge silver wire. Burn balls on one end of each of the wires. Thread the wire into the center area of the necklace.

9 Place beads on the wire, then continue to insert the wires into the other side of the silver piece on the necklace (see figure 1). Complete all three before moving on.

10 Move the beads toward the side with the balled wire ends. Hold the necklace with the pliers on the inside of the necklace, securing the beads away from the flame you'll be using.

11 Place the three wire ends into the torch to burn balls on the ends on each.

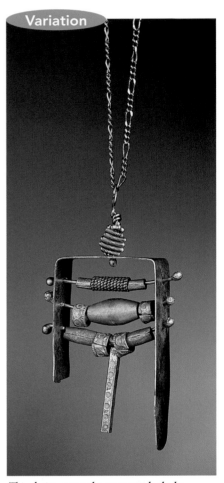

This design can take on many looks by adding a variety of beads.

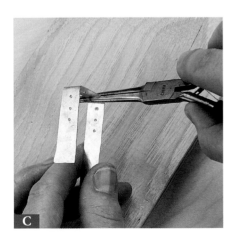

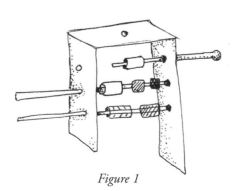

Figure 1

Moving Parts Necklace and Earrings

12 Repeat steps 8 through 11 for the earrings, only cut the two wire pieces at ⅞ inch (2.2 cm). You can also choose to use beads (as with the necklace) or different matching pieces, such as the silver triangles shown in the example in the photo on page 102.

13 Cut two pieces of the 18-gauge wire 3 inches (7.6 cm) long for the earrings and one piece 5 to 6 inches (12.7 to 15.2 cm) long for the necklace. These connect the pieces to their findings. Burn one end on each piece of wire to make balls form. Insert the wire pieces into the top center holes

from the inside out through the top. The balled wire ends will keep the wire from going all the way through (see figure 2).

14 Thread on a bead (if desired), and finish by making a wrapped loop on each of the earrings and the necklace (see photo D).

15 Open the ear wires to thread on the earrings and then close them. Thread the neck chain through the hoop to finish the necklace.

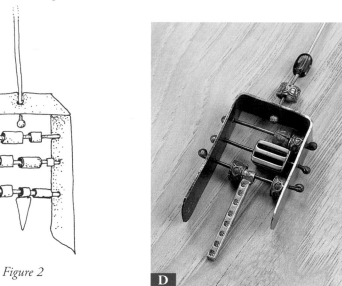

Figure 2

D

Variation

Bend the metal differently to achieve other shapes in this design.

Copper and Silver Bangle Bracelet

In this project, small pieces of forged copper, silver and copper jump rings, and a variety of beads assembled together create an eye-catching bracelet. Using variations on metals, materials, and embellishments will make each bracelet unique.

Copper and Silver Bangle Bracelet

TECHNIQUES

Applying heat-treated patinas
Burning balls on wire ends
Making wire-wrapped loops
Embellishing wire with bead techniques
Attaching jump rings

MATERIALS

Sheeting:
Copper, 24-gauge, 4 x 5 inches (10.2 x 12.7 cm)

Wire:
Copper, 20-gauge, 6 feet (1.8 m)

Findings and embellishments:
Silver head pins, 20-gauge, 2½ inches (6.4 cm) long

16 to 20 each of 10 or more different kinds of copper and silver beads

17 to 22 silver jump rings, 20-or 18-gauge

50 to 70 copper jump rings, 20- or 18-gauge

1 copper claw toggle

TOOLS

Propane torch
Pliers
Sheet metal cutters
Hammer
Anvil
Metal hole punch tool
Safety glasses
Leather glove
Scissors
Liver of sulphur

WHAT YOU DO

1 Before you cut the individual pieces, heat a 4 x 5-inch (10.2 x 12.7 cm) copper sheet with a torch. This produces a patina from the heat and makes it easier to cut all the small pieces. Cut the sheet into small rectangles. Do not try to make them all the same, but vary the width and lengths (see photo A). You will need 32 to 40 pieces, each approximately ¼ inch (0.6 cm) wide and ½ to 1¼ inches (1.3 to 3.2 cm) long.

2 Hammer the cut pieces on the anvil. Because they are small, you can only hold onto a small corner of the copper as you forge the metal. Allow the shape to become distorted and have a deckled edge. Be sure that you don't thin the copper out too much from hammering. Once you are done, lay the pieces out, positioning them to balance the shapes throughout the bracelet.

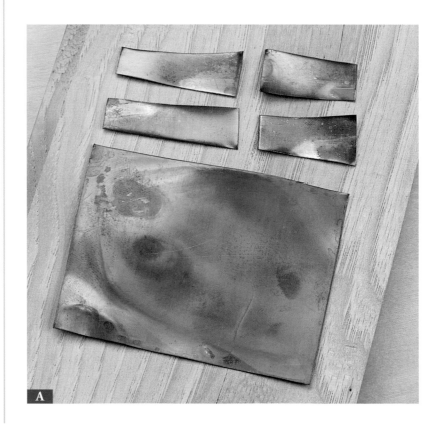

A

3 You will need two pieces of copper for each connection or silver jump ring. One piece of copper per connection will have one hole punched in one end. The other piece of copper will have holes at each end of the rectangle shape. Decide what pieces will have either one or two holes throughout the bracelet, and lay them back in order.

4 Cut the 20-gauge copper wire into 3-inch (7.6 cm) pieces, the same number as you have copper pieces. Burn one of the ends on each piece, and prepare them by using a cold-water patina to create red balls.

5 Assemble the pieces for the bracelet by following the steps below. There are three separate components that group together at each jump ring connection. Once you begin the series of three, repeat it throughout the bracelet:

• First, connect the copper pieces with two punched holes to the bracelet by a copper jump ring placed in one of the two holes. In the other hole, make a bead embellishment using a pattern of three to five beads and a wrapped loop (see figure 1). Repeat the same bead pattern as you progress through the bracelet.

• Second, use the copper pieces with one hole to connect to the bracelet with a wrapped loop. Add a bead for embellishment (see figure 2). Use the same type of bead for all of these connections.

• Third, the final bangle to be added to the series of connections will be a silver head pin that has beads threaded onto it to create a bangle (see figure 3). Again, repeat the same pattern on all the silver head pins in the bracelet. Finish the head pin bangle by making a wrapped loop to make the bracelet connection.

Figure 1

Figure 2

Figure 3

Copper and Silver Bangle Bracelet

Instead of the irregular, aged-looking shapes of the main project, this bracelet uses the same techniques to reach a rounder, brighter design.

6 Once you've completed the entire bracelet's components, you are ready to assemble the bracelet. Photo B shows the three types of components you will put together. First, securely close all the copper jump rings if any are open or separated. Then open the silver jump rings by sliding them side to side. Thread on two copper jump rings and one set of the three bangle components (see photo C).

7 Continue to assemble the bracelet by opening the second silver jump ring and threading on the second set of components and two copper jump rings (see photo D). Connect it to the first set by inserting a open silver jump ring into the copper jump rings on the initial silver jump ring and then closing it.

8 Continue to add on each set of three. On the third connection, follow the same steps except alternate the copper rings in their order with the set of three. By doing this, the bangles will alternate on each side of the bracelet and make it balanced as shown.

9 Continue the same process throughout the entire length of the bracelet. Once you've created this pattern, you can see many possibilities for other options. When you reach your desired length, finish the bracelet on its last additions by replacing the two copper jump rings with the copper claw clasp (see photo E).

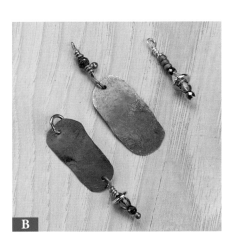

B

C

D

E

Bead Pod Pin

This simple pin was adopted from a Japanese packaging technique traditionally used to wrap eggs safely. The secure wrapping lends itself as a wonderful way to hold and display these beads. The tying method used is not exactly a weaving technique, but it is a great fiber application that translates very well into wire.

TECHNIQUES
Wrapping and tying

MATERIALS

Sheeting:
Stainless mesh screen - 2 x 4 inches (5.1 x 10.2 cm)

Wire:
Silver, 18-gauge, 30 inches (75 cm)
Silver, 24-gauge, 6 feet (1.8 m)

Findings and embellishments:
5 to 7 assorted beads
Stickpin with a flat end area

TOOLS

Scissors or wire cutters
Needle-nose pliers
Torch
Fast-setting cyanoacrylate glue

WHAT YOU DO

1 Cut six 5-inch (12.7 cm) pieces of the 18-gauge silver wire. With the torch, prepare the ends of wire by burning balls and prepare the mesh with heat to give it color.

2 Hold the six spokes about 1 inch (2.5 cm) from the end. Anchor the 6-foot (1.8 m) length of 24-gauge silver wire by wrapping it back over itself. Leave the short end of the 24-gauge wire toward the long ends of the 18-gauge wire (see figure 1).

3 Next, wrap the end on itself to secure the 24-gauge wire. Continue to wrap about three to four more times (see figure 2). Open up the spoke wires on one side to make a boat shape. Include the short 24-gauge wire in this group.

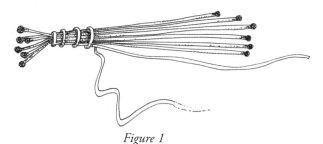

Figure 1

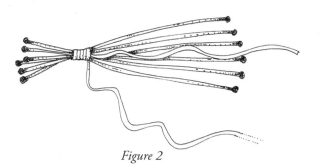

Figure 2

Bead Pod Pin

4 Fold the mesh in about 1/16 inch (0.16 cm) on the two long sides to eliminate the raw sharp edge (see photo A).

5 Taper the mesh down on each end to avoid some of the bulk. Cup it in the wire like a boat, and bend the mesh to fit in the boat shape. Place the 24-gauge wire on top of the mesh in the bottom of the boat shape (see photo B).

6 Wrap the same way, but this time catch the end of the mesh. Wrap it in securely. Secure the end wrap by looping the 24-gauge wire on itself in the front of the pod, and place the 24-gauge wire over the opening of the pod shape (see figures 3 and 4).

7 String the beads on the short piece of 24-gauge wire inside the cupped mesh area. Bend the end of the wire to avoid having the beads fall off as you work. You can create variation in size from smaller at the ends and larger in the center to create a nice, tight fit and a true pod shape (see figure 5).

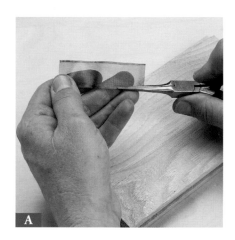

A

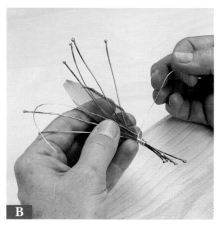

B

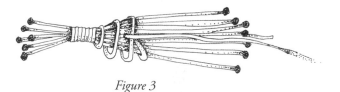

Figure 3

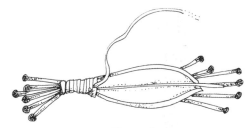

Figure 4

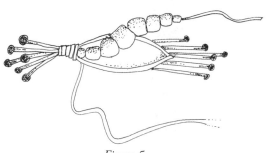

Figure 5

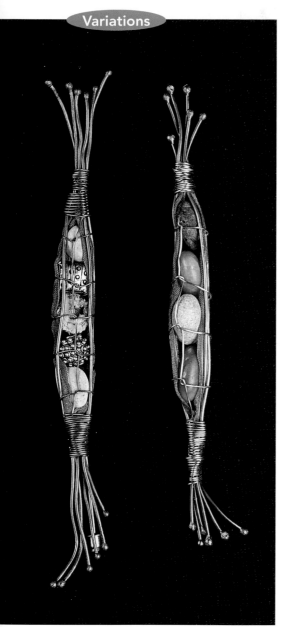

Try another metal and add pebbles, small items, and natural beads to give your pins a variety of looks.

8 Shape and mold the wires around the beads tightly and securely (see photo C). Place the spoke wires where you want them. Slide the stick-pin in between the 18-gauge spokes, and glue the back to the mesh. Let it dry (see photo D). I usually try to glue this a little toward one end so it will hang nicely.

9 Place the long wrapping wire straight across the front of the opening with the beads. With the pliers,

C

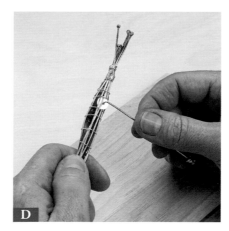

D

bend the wire where you want the tie to be. You will usually have five or more connections, so space them accordingly (see figure 6).

10 Bring the wire around the bead pod, and catch the bent area and pull tight. Do this approximately five times (or whatever fits in your space) along the entire bead pod.

11 End the bead pod by once again gathering all the mesh and spoke wires together. Finish by wrapping the 24-gauge wire tightly. Secure the end by threading it back through a small area of the wrap (see figure 7).

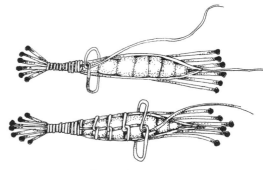

Figure 6

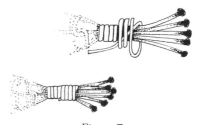

Figure 7

Stitched Segments Pin

Just by taking an uneven square, cutting it on the diagonal, altering its shape and texture, and stitching it back together, you can create an intriguing contemporary pin. The simple coiling stitch used to connect the piece together is a basketry technique that can make for a great addition of detail to a piece of jewelry.

TECHNIQUES

Applying liver of sulphur or silver/black patina
Forging wire to create paddles
Stitching: figure 8 and wrap method

MATERIALS

Sheeting:
Silver, 24-gauge, 1½ x 2½ inches (3.8 x 6.4 cm)

Wire:
Silver, 18-gauge, 3 inches (7.6 cm)
Silver, 26-gauge, 5 feet (1.5 m)

Findings and embellishments:
Silver pin back, 1½ inches (3.8 cm) long with holes

TOOLS

Sheet metal cutters
Hammer
Anvil
Liver of sulphur or silver/black
Awl
Brass brush or bench polisher
Hole punch for metal

WHAT YOU DO

1 Cut a square of silver sheeting from one corner to the opposite to create two triangles with rounded corners as shown in the main photo. Hammer the squares to make the surface smooth, and hammer the edges further to create a deckled effect (see photo A).

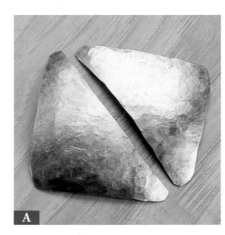

A

B

2 On the front side of the piece, treat it with the liver of sulphur or silver/black to darken the entire surface black. Use the awl and hammer on the opposite side to texture the pieces.

3 Using the brass brush or bench polisher, brush the front surface to expose the bumps made by the awl (see photo B). Expose the silver on the edges by brushing away the black.

4 Measure and cut the 18-gauge silver wire to extend between the two triangles, reaching about ¼ inch (0.6 cm) past each end. Forge the ends of the wire to create paddles (see photo C).

C

Stitched Segments Pin

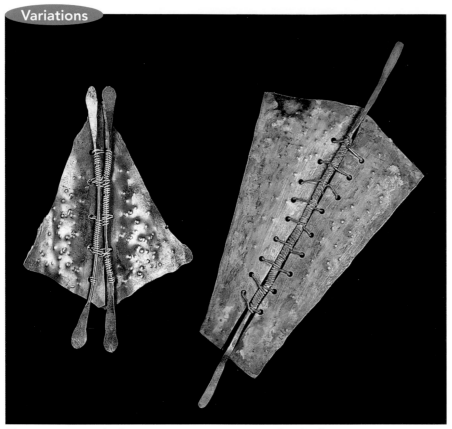

Try using copper, multiple connecting wires, or patinas to alter this design.

5 With the metal punch, make seven to nine holes on either side of the connection area. The holes should be directly across from each other on each piece and approximately ¼ inch (0.6 cm) apart and ⅛ inch (0.3 cm) from the edge (see figure 1).

6 Burn one end of the 26-gauge silver wire to create a ball. Start the stitching process by threading the wire from the back side to the front on one of the end holes (see figure 2).

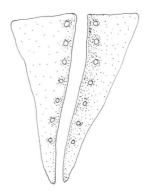

Figure 1

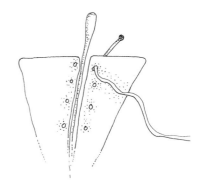

Figure 2

7 Proceed to stitch the two pieces together by first looping around the middle wire piece one time and then stitching to the other piece of silver also in its end hole (see photo D). Then wrap the thin, 24-gauge silver wire tightly and evenly around the 18-gauge wire until you have reached another set of holes to stitch into.

8 When you reach the second set of holes directly across from one another, stitch into each one. Make sure that you connect with a loop around the center 18-gauge wire piece (see figures 3 and 4). Continue this process until you reach the last holes in the row. Do not cut or end the 24-gauge wire piece.

9 Attach the pin back by threading the wire up the back side under the stitching (see photo E). Stitch the pin back on by sewing in and out of the holes on the pin back. End the piece of wire by tucking the end securely into the stitching, and cut closely to avoid a sharp end.

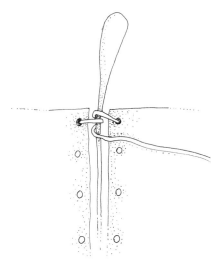

Figure 3

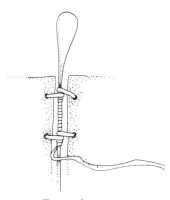

Figure 4

Twisted Wire Choker Necklace

With simple twists and beads, this project will come to life in no time. Depending on how you arrange the vine and where you add tendrils, this technique can take on many looks. Delicate vines and tendrils dotted with seed beads will make this a favorite style that can be interpreted into rings, bracelets, and earrings.

TECHNIQUES
Twisting wire

MATERIALS

Wire:
Copper, 26-gauge, 50 feet (15.2 m)

Findings and embellishments:
10 grams or more of seed beads all one color or in various colors, sizes, and designs

TOOLS
Scissors
Needle-nose pliers

WHAT YOU DO

1 Cut a 5-foot (1.5 m) length of the 26-gauge copper wire. You'll be working in more pieces of this length a number of times in the project. Thread five beads on the wire then bend the wire in half, placing the beads in the bend, and twist. This creates the look of a small flower (see figure 1).

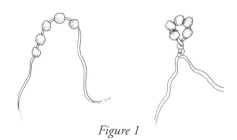

Figure 1

2 Twist a small section on the two wires then thread five more beads on one of the ends, and follow the same procedure of twisting (see photo A). Keep making these vine-like twisted shapes (see photo B). The only rules are to always have a two-twisted wire area, and never have a single wire showing.

3 Add a new wire by twisting a new end into the existing vines (see photo C).

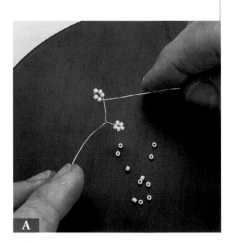

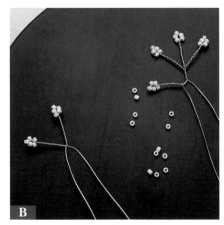

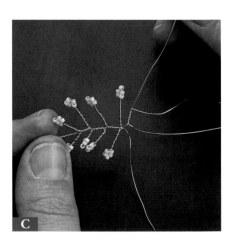

Twisted Wire Choker Necklace

4 You can put added tendrils on separately (see photo D).

5 You can make the connection in the back by wrapping the wire into a hook shape and hooking it to the vine at your desired length, or you can lash a commercial hook on with wire.

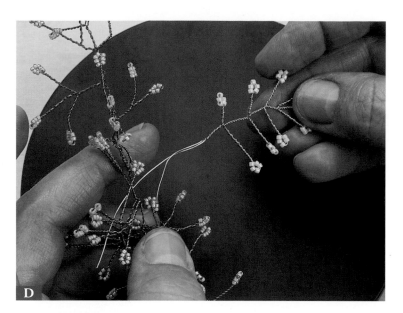

D

Twist a cluster of beads together, then use the ends to wire wrap a band for a ring.

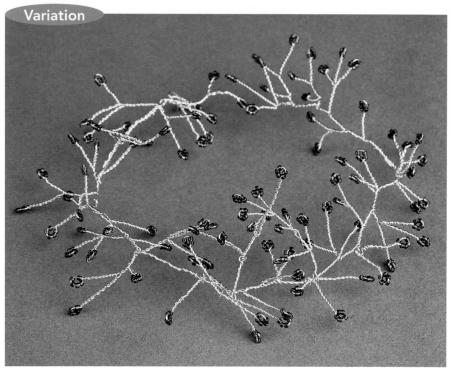

Change the beads and the wire for a whole new look.

Gallery

Left: Julia Lowther
Persian Wave Necklace, 2005
43 x 1.3 x 1.3 cm
Sterling silver, hand linked
Photo by Daniel Van Rossen

Below left: Edna Kuhta
Split Planet, 2006
12 x 10.5 x 1 cm
Copper, fine silver; textured,
cold connected, fold formed,
hydraulic pressed
Photo by Chris Kuhta

Below right: Judith Hoyt
Red and Gray Head Necklace,
2003
6.4 x 10.2 cm
Copper, found metal; riveted
Photo by John Lenz

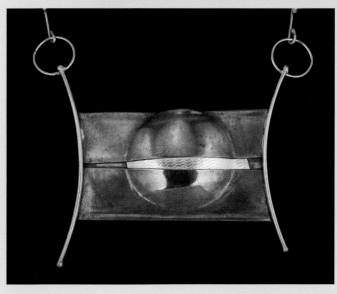

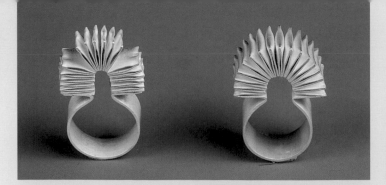

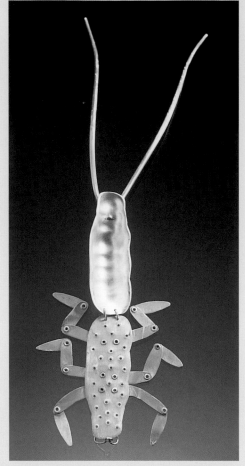

Top left: Suzanne Esser
Untitled, 2006
Left, 3.9 x 2.2 x 0.9 cm; right, 3.4 x 2.6 x 0.9 cm
Silver; folded
Photo by Marte Visser

Center left: Alysia A. Fischer
Locust Wings, 2005
Each: 3.3 x 2.1 x 2.2 cm
Brass, sterling silver; roller printed, hand cut,
cold connected, riveted
Photo by Jeffrey A. Sabo

Bottom left: Roberta and David Williamson
Petie Pins, 2004
Each: 5.5 x 5.5 x 1.2 cm
Sterling silver, beach stones; hand sawed,
bezel set, drilled, wrapped
Photo by Jerry Anthony

Top right: Valerie A. Heck
Bug Tea Infuser, 2003
2.5 x 5 x 14.3 cm
Sterling silver; formed, forged, soldered,
riveted, cold connected, hand cut, hinged
Photo by artist

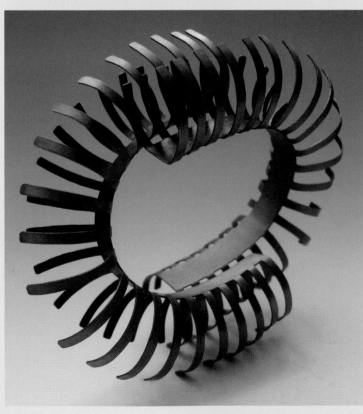

Top left: Hu Jun
Untitled, 2007
11.5 x 6.5 x 1 cm
Brass, silver, lacquer; riveted, painted, cold connected
Photo by artist

Bottom left: Yuh-Shyuan Chen
Interlace, 2007
3.4 x 11.3 x 9.7 cm
Copper; hand cut
Photo by artist

Top right: Diane Falkenhagen
Rococo Landscape Brooch, 2006
5.7 x 9.2 x 1 cm
Sterling silver, mixed media, 14-karat gold, 23-karat gold leaf, nuts, bolts; fabricated, cold connected, riveted
Photo by Bill Pogue

Bottom right: Zee Galliano
Domed Earrings, 2006
6.4 x 2.5 x 0.6 cm
Sterling silver, copper; textured, domed, riveted
Photo by artist

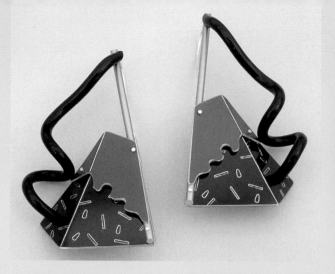

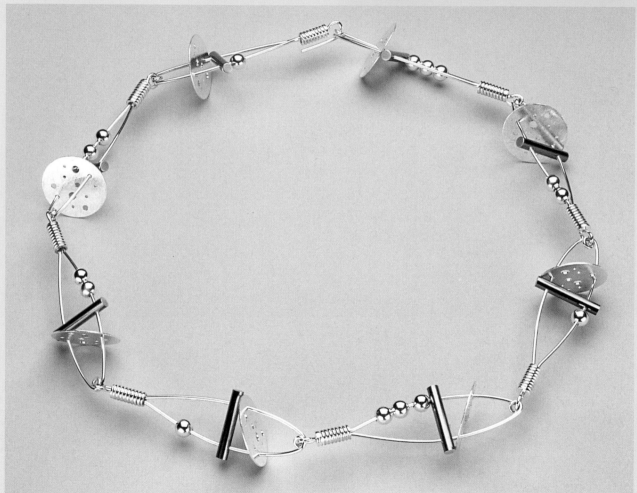

Top left: Debra Lynn Gold
Untitled, 1999
5 x 3 x 1 cm
Colored aluminum, sterling silver,
dyed vinyl; hand engraved, riveted
Photo by artist

Top right: Jason C. Morrissey
Linkage Studies, 2006
Center piece, 4 x 5.5 x 2 cm
Copper, silver, brass; forged,
roller milled
Photo by Robert Diamante

Bottom: Debra Lynn Gold
Stirred Collar, 2004
15 x 15 x 2 cm
Sterling silver, colored aluminum;
pierced, hand-applied distressed finish,
tension strung
Photo by Sue Ann Kuhn Smith

Top left: Hyeseung Shin
Cold Joint Necklace, 2003
20 x 1.5 x 0.2 cm
Sterling silver; fabricated, riveted
Photo by Munch Studio

Top right: Jane Bowden
Woven Bangle, 2006
10 x 7.5 x 3 cm
Sterling silver; hand woven, cold worked
Photo by Grant Hancock

Center right: Jeanie Pratt
Una Ala, 2007
10 x 15 x 1 cm
Copper, niobium, sterling silver, brass, opal, patina; looped, anodized, roller printed, etched, cold connected, riveted, bolted
Photo by Carol Holaday

Bottom right: E. Douglas Wunder
Untitled, 2007
12 x 12 x 3 cm
Titanium, sterling silver; hand cut, anodized, constructed, cold connected, riveted
Photo by Larry Sanders

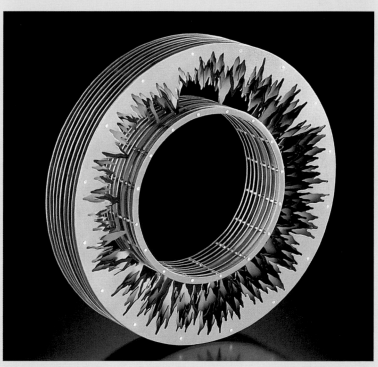

Index of Gallery Artists

Dedication

This book is dedicated to these six special women who have encouraged and supported me throughout my life:

My grandmothers, Lillian and Cora, whose eternal spirits live in my heart

My cousin, Laura, whose own talents and perseverance inspire me

My sister, Martha, whose love and dedication are my constant support

My mother, Margaret, who is the strength in my life and the voice on my shoulder

My daughter, Abbey, who is my light, my love, my life, my Abbey

Thank you all for who you are.

Acknowledgments

Thanks to Lark Books, and particularly to Carol Taylor, President and Publisher, for another opportunity to work with such a great group of people.

A very heartfelt thanks to Marthe Le Van, Senior Editor, whose tremendous support and encouragement have been instrumental in both the conception and completion of this book. You are truly a generous person with your friendship, words, and talents. Thanks also to Larry Shea, Editor, whose organizational skills, editing talents, and attention to detail have made this not only a great book but a very enjoyable journey.

It has been a privilege to have Kathy Holmes, the book's art director, lend her artistic flavor and creative talents to the layout, photography setup, and gallery section of this book. I was also thrilled to have a second opportunity to work with Stewart O'Shields, the book's photographer. You are such an amazing artist. My work always looks the best when you create an image of it.

Thanks to Cindy LaBreacht for the beautiful cover design. I also appreciate the work Jess Clarke did in proofreading the book. Thanks to Jeff Hamilton, Shannon Yokeley, Avery Johnson, and Travis Medford for their art production assistance and to Kathleen McCafferty, Amanda Carestio, and Mark Bloom for their editorial assistance.

Special thanks to my family members, dear friends, and to my art community, where I have found lifelong friendships, genuine support, and heartfelt hugs. The endless laughter, love and memories are irreplaceable.

Finally, I want to thank my son, Logan, for hanging in there and working hard even when his mom is off to another part of the world. You are an exceptional young man with unlimited potential and you are growing up so fast. I am so proud to call you my son. Thanks to my daughter, Abbey; without your support, I could never achieve my goals. I appreciate all that you are and cannot imagine life without you. Lastly, I want to thank my husband Bob for being an incredible partner in life. You never stop surprising me. Thank you for keeping our lives interesting, passionate, and full.

About the Author

Mary Hettmansperger is a mixed-media fiber and jewelry artist with a focus on basketry, metals, and quilting. She has been teaching and exhibiting her artwork full-time for 25 years, across the United States and abroad. She teaches workshops and classes in many venues, including Arrowmont Craft School, the Bead & Button Show, Convergence, fiber and bead shops, art and craft schools, and a number of other conferences, guilds, and retreats.

Mary's work has been published in numerous books, including *Beading with Crystals, Fiber Design 7, 500 Baskets, Creative Scarecrows, Teapots: Makers & Collectors,* and *Fabulous Jewelry from Found Objects.* She is the author and illustrator of the book *Fabulous Woven Jewelry* (Lark, 2005). Mary also has had her work published in several magazines, including *Beadwork, Art Jewelry, Bead & Button, Shuttle Spindle & Dyepot,* and *Crafts Report.* She has appeared on several segments for the PBS television programs *Beads Baubles and Jewels* and *The Art of Quilting.* Mary exhibits her work at SOFA with the Katie Gingrass Gallery and at various art shows and galleries throughout the United States.

Index